The Unheralded
Majority

The Unheralded Majority

Contemporary Women as Mothers

Lydia N. O'Donnell
Wellesley College

Lexington Books
D.C. Heath and Company/Lexington, Massachusetts/Toronto

Library of Congress Cataloging in Publication Data

O'Donnell, Lydia, 1949-
  The unheralded majority.

  Includes index.
  1. Mothers—Massachusetts—Boston Metropolitan Area—Case studies. 2. Mothers—Employment—Massachusetts—Boston Metropolitan Area—Case studies. 3. Family—Massa-chusetts—Boston Metropolitan Area—Case studies. 4. Voluntarism—Massachusetts—Boston Metropolitan Area—Case studies. 5. Sex role—Massachusetts—Boston Metropolitan Area—Case studies. I. Title.
  HQ759.3235   1985   305.4'2   83-49530
  ISBN 0-669-08274-0 (alk. paper)

Published simultaneously in Canada
Printed in the United States of America on acid-free paper
International Standard Book Number: 0-669-08274-0
Library of Congress Catalog Card Number: 83-49530

This book is dedicated to the mothers who donated their valuable time in order to help us understand what it means to be a woman and mother in modern times. They have not only helped me in my work as a researcher, but more importantly, they have made me realize the importance of slowing down and saving time so that I could truly appreciate my own early years of motherhood.

Contents

Tables

Acknowledgments

Research for this book was funded by the National Science Foundation, Grant No. DAR-7910358; the principal investigator was Laura Lein. I want to take this opportunity to thank colleagues at the Wellesley College Center for Research on Women for their encouragement and, in particular, Ann Stueve for her valuable and provocative suggestions, criticism, and advice. As members of my dissertation committee at Harvard University, Sara Lawrence Lightfoot and Mary Jo Bane guided the research and shared their knowledge and insights. The often very lengthy interviews could not have been completed without the efforts of research assistants Christina Pershing and Diana Taylor. Jan Putnam and Helen Matthew were an invaluable source of help in preparing the final manuscript.

I also wish to credit my husband, Carl, for the many hours he spent editing initial drafts and encouraging me to reach my goal. This project could not have been completed without his unwavering support. Finally, I thank my son, Blake, who has helped me understand what other mothers mean by the pleasures, joys, and difficulties of child rearing and whose patience and forbearance over the first three years of his life enabled me to experience the best of both mothering and employment—despite his heartfelt comment on one particularly harried day: "Mommy, I want to take your chapters and throw them up in the clouds so that they never come down again."

Part I
Presenting the Study

Introduction:
Toward a New Synthesis

This is a book about contemporary mothers, their lives, families, and the communities in which they live. It is not about those visible and vocal minorities who often capture our attention, such as the few women who have reached the pinnacles of success and wealth in professional careers; nor is it about those less powerful minorities who get labeled and studied as "social problems," teenage mothers, single-parents who are barely surviving the hardships imposed by the current economy, and so on. Rather, it is the story of parents and children in the mainstream of the United States, that part of the population referred to by Wilensky and other scholars as the "middle mass."[1] It is about women who feel that they have some degree of choice and control over the course of their lives, but who also recognize that their days are shaped, and at times constrained, both by the needs of their children and husbands and by the opportunities for friendship, employment, and child-rearing support available within their local communities.

In many ways, this is an account of how family and community life have carried on despite fears and apprehensions surrounding the well-publicized statistics on dwindling birth rates, the increasing number of marriages which end in divorce, and the dramatic rise in women's employment. Unfortunately, media headlines and our tendency to focus on what is changing and novel rather than on what remains the same have overshadowed a number of basic facts: most women still become mothers; most children are raised for most of their lives in nuclear families; and most families continue to participate actively in the social life of their communities.

The seventy-four women interviewed for this study lived with their families in two working- and middle-class towns, both located in the Boston metropolitan area. (The names of the respondents and of the two towns have been changed to protect their anonymity.) The families described here are neither rich nor poor; they worry about rising costs and making ends meet, yet they are able to afford those few extras and luxuries which can make life more pleasant. There is something almost stereotypical about them. Parents', and particularly mothers', lives still do revolve around caring for children when they are ill, sharing their problems and joys, shopping, cooking family meals, locating the "right" nursery school, joining the PTA, attending teacher conferences, and the myriad other tasks and activities which are part of child rearing in our society. This account will strike chords reminiscent of the many earlier studies of families residing in communities such as Levittown, Crestwood Heights, Elmstown, and Middletown.[2] Like these older community studies, and unlike much of the more specific, fragmented, and service-oriented research of recent years, this book takes a broad view. It describes the daily lives of children and their mothers, and examines the links between families and the local community. In part, then, this is a study of continuity, of how children continue to shape the lives of their parents and of how women, as mothers, continue to play an active role in shaping the nature of family and community life.

The mothers who participated in this research are best described as mainstream. They are not the pioneers who fought hard to enter traditionally male occupations; they are not radical feminists who reject the idea of marriage and children; they are not the 1970s "Supermoms" who balanced glamorous, high-status jobs with their parenting and domestic chores. Instead, they are, in the vast majority of cases, like most mothers in our country today—low paid "pink collar" workers, secretaries, clerks, nurses, teachers, and full-time homemakers. This does not mean, however, that their lives have been untouched by social and demographic changes or that they see themselves as mere carbon copies of their own mothers, for this is also a study of social change. Indeed, what I describe in the following pages began as an investigation of how economic conditions and changing social mores have affected the nature of our families and communities as well as the ambitions, motivations, and commitments of modern mothers. Listening to how women talk about their own lives and how they recount the activities of their children and spouses, I wanted to learn how the rhetoric, ideologies, and realities of recent social changes, and specifically changing women's roles, have filtered through and been experienced by mainstream U.S. families.

Mothers' Work: A Reevaluation

At the outset of my research, in the late 1970s, my perspective largely reflected that of the professional community of which I am a part. I was primarily interested in identifying the types of constraints and obstacles women face because of their continuing role as the primary caretakers of our nation's children. I hoped to suggest through my work what types of social policies and support services could be implemented to free women of their domestic roles and enable them to compete more equitably with men in arenas other than the home and family. My approach was not unusual: it was typical of how most feminists, and more generally, of how we as a society have perceived of the tradeoffs between domestic life and the world of employment. Feminist, feminist-Marxist, and even more moderate analyses of the apparently different worlds of women have shared an emphasis on the costs and sacrifices mothers bear because of their involvement in child rearing.[3] Through such a lens, it becomes all too easy to view women merely as victims and captives of their domestic work and thus to discount women's commitments to what we think of as traditional roles—as mothers, homemakers, and community volunteers—as expressions of naiveté and oppression. In keeping with this portrait, the future seemed evident: given opportunities and access to male bastions of power and influence, women would be freed from their servitude to so-called "women's work" and eager to seek achievements and satisfactions elsewhere.

Two experiences, however, made me realize that such a perspective was outdated, limited, and condescending. The first was my exposure to the mothers who kindly agreed to be interviewed, often in depth and at length, for the study. The second, coinciding with the first and, at least in my own mind forever entwined, was the birth of my own first child and my personal entrance into the community of mothers. The women I met through my interviews and in my own early days of child rearing forced me to reassess many of my original biases and rethink what it means to be a woman and mother in modern times. They made me realize the deep satisfactions of mothering as well as the stresses, and they helped me appreciate that children are young only for a short time and that the years women spend child rearing can provide pleasures and rewards which are difficult to incorporate in any formal cost-benefit analysis of the tradeoffs between employment and family life.

Costs versus Benefits

The women I came into contact with both as friends and as interview subjects spoke out strongly and passionately about the importance of "being there" for their families, about the wisdom of taking time off or limiting paid jobs so that employment does not interfere with family life, and about what they perceived as the myth of "quality time." The mothers felt that, at least in part, it is the quantity of time spent with children and put into maintaining homes, families, and communities which is crucial; through their words and deeds they expressed their feeling that quantity of time in itself begets quality. Contrary to those who argue that women must sacrifice their own needs and identities to devote even a portion of their lives to mothering, these women did not view such investments as being selfless or personally unrewarding. Instead, they spoke eloquently and at length about the importance of mothering, both because of what children gain from maternal care, and significantly, because of what women gain from being with children. In addition, the women called attention to the importance of the many subtle and often time-consuming extensions of mothering, including the work women do to support their extended families and to ensure that their neighborhoods and communities remain vital and vibrant places which, in turn, can be counted on to support nuclear family life.

Most of all, the women helped me understand that contemporary mothers have not all been caught in the so-called trap of motherhood. Rather, most of the women I came to know are aware of the immediate and long-term sacrifices they are making to invest so much in tending children. Moreover, most had been employed for years before giving birth and the majority expect to continue paid work, although on a limited basis, even while their children are young. They recognize the rewards and status accorded to those who bring home paychecks, and they derive a good deal of satisfaction from their paid jobs and careers. They join with more outspoken feminists in hoping that time spent child rearing will eventually become less costly in terms of career sacrifices. However, despite their awareness of the tradeoffs they are making, virtually all have made family work their first priority—at least for the time they expect to be raising young children.

As I listened to women's accounts of what they derive from mothering, I came to recognize not only the strength of their commitments to families and communities, but also the extent to which we have taken so much of mothers' work for granted. What I was hearing was the voice of a quiet and unheralded majority. Despite their emphasis on home and family, these modern mothers are not mere anachronisms, throwbacks to a previous era. Instead, they are women who have benefitted from many aspects of the women's movement. Yet they have also rejected the notion that time devoted to mothering is unnecessary, wasteful of their talents, or unsatisfying. They are women who feel they have had the opportunity to consider different ways of combining work and family and to act upon their values and understanding of what is important in life.

In large part because of the social and economic upheavals of the 1960s and 1970s, women are now gaining the strength and vision to speak out about what truly matters in their lives. In the process of doing so, they are discovering that they do not, in the words of one mother I spoke with, "want to buy into a male vision of the world." Rather, these mainstream women are arriving at a new synthesis, a creative reformulation of past and present views of women's work. They are redefining what is important for themselves.

As a result of my experiences with these mothers, therefore, rather than maintaining my initial focus on the constraints and difficulties imposed by child rearing, I have become more interested in presenting this synthesis, in letting others hear how such women talk about the importance of mothering and employment in their lives. As Carol Gilligan, the author of *In a Different Voice,* has argued, women, to a greater degree than men, judge their actions and frame their commitments in terms of their responsibilities to others.[4] I have been repeatedly impressed by the extent to which the women I have met and many others like them have been able to resist the tendency to equate personal worth or real work with a salary. With little external support or encouragement, they have continued to place a high value on their unpaid family and community work and on their responsibility to create an acceptable quality of life for their loved ones and themselves. This is not to suggest that they envision motherhood as totally encompassing their lives or fulfilling all their hopes and ambitions. First, mothering is no longer looked on as a life-long occupation; it essentially lasts for that limited number of years young children are in a household. Second, jobs and other outside involvements clearly have assumed an important place in women's lives; in itself, this is a striking ramification and reminder of the debt contemporary mothers owe to the women's movement. However, it is essential to understand that even as they are beginning to make their ways into new arenas which emphasize the importance of individual striving and achievement, mothers have retained their deeply felt notions of responsibility for the care and nurturance of others.

There are some who will argue that they do so only at a cost to themselves; that is, in continuing to frame their lives in terms of the needs of others, in particular their family members, women sacrifice not only career success but their individual identities. Clinical case reports indicate that there are indeed some women who lose themselves amidst their family entanglements, and a few of the women interviewed did fear a loss of identity through their immersion in the maternal role. But in focusing primarily on such cases, we can lose sight of the strength of many women. There are dangers to a perspective which places its emphasis on the importance of personal relations, but there is also the potential for great satisfaction, for a synthesis, as it were, of the selfless and the selfish. Women today have the opportunity to consider not just what being a mother demands of an individual, but what it returns. Thus, they resist the tendency to view life choices in terms of dichotomies, a what's good for them versus what's good for me. Despite an acknowledgement of many of the everyday tradeoffs between one's individual desires and the needs of others, women are finding out that is possible to learn as much, if not more, about "me" through intimate relations with children and involvement in the maternal role as it is in other fields of human endeavor. Contrary to models which imply that individuals can only attain a sense of accomplishment and self-worth through paid work, the women I spoke with talked of the achievements and sense of a job well done they gained from their unpaid efforts at home and in their communities.

The New Synthesis

In the following chapters I illustrate how, in the midst of social changes, women have not passively accepted the singular importance of employment and one life-long career. Observing the binds of their husbands and fathers, they feel this is not all there is to life. Rather, women are striving to find new ways of integrating paid and unpaid work, of interweaving family, employment, and community involvements, which enable them to forge a sense of personal worth and effectiveness with an awareness of the importance of responsibility and commitment to others. This is the vital part of what I mean by the new synthesis.

I believe this study provides evidence that women are actors who are charged with incorporating motherhood into their lives in ways which are acceptable to them as individuals but which also ensure that much critical work, for both families and communities, continues to get done. An emphasis on the constraints on women's lives was instrumental in opening and expanding opportunities, and it is clear that many women are still caught in gender-assigned situations which prevent them from realizing their potential and taking advantage of new pathways. One only has to read the disheartening statistics on the feminization of poverty, on male–female pay differentials, and the like, to realize that we still must continue to tear down barriers which force so many women to pay stiff penalties because of their family responsibilities. Yet, at this point in time, an emphasis on constraints is not sufficient. In addition to continuing the struggle to remove obstacles from women's lives (especially from those who are not as fortunate as the mothers who participated in this study), we must also consider more explicitly what women themselves want from their lives and what they value. This is neither to deny that constraints still exist nor to ignore the fact that life choices always involve tradeoffs and foresaken opportunities. However, it is time to realize that the women's movement has provided today's mothers with more than the chance to get out of their homes. It has also given them the impetus to reconsider their lives and their possibilities. As a result, there is an awareness of options that was not previously available, and it is within this context that women act on their values and beliefs to construct their lives and life's work.

In large part due to the women's movement and its discussion of sex roles, contemporary mothers recognize that the years they devote to child rearing are only one part of their multifaceted lives. Fully employed for years before having children, they expect to reenter full-time employment at some point in the future. Therefore, instead of feeling trapped by motherhood, they look on their time as child rearers as productive, valuable, and more often than not, immensely personally rewarding—despite their awareness of the economic sacrifices they make to be primary child-care providers and despite their knowledge of such threats as divorce and its subsequent economic upheaval. Unfortunately, few have given women credit for this positive recognition of their life course or their ability to anticipate and deal with life transitions. For example, although researchers such as Grace Baruch and Rosalind Barnett have drawn our attention to the satisfactions women in midlife experience as their days of child rearing come to an end and employment and careers take on new significance, we still tend to focus on the difficulties of midlife transitions and women's apprehensions about the time when children are grown.[5] Certainly, no one can deny that many women have experienced problems adjusting to a life without children, to a divorce, or to the death of a husband. But, once again, clinical portraits of women in trouble or crisis may not be the most accurate guides to understanding how a majority of contemporary women face their lives or plan for the future.[6]

In updating our account of women's lives, this book presents a revised image of motherhood by examining what women value and what they do. I address what we as a society stand to gain from women's work and from acknowledging the perspective of mainstream women and their synthesis of old and new roles and values. I highlight women's recognition of their responsibility to the web of human interactions, from relations inside the nuclear family to participation in the larger community. I do not argue that women are uniquely qualified to be child rearers, but that women recognize, often despite pressures to the contrary, the importance of their unpaid family and community work, the reasons why it need be continued, and the reasons why paid services cannot necessarily be counted on to supplant a parent's involvement and personal efforts.

In responding to this new synthesis, we will be forced to confront many difficult questions we have heretofore been reluctant to face. For example, how do we as individuals, as feminists, and as a society view and support the choices of mainstream U.S. women? Why have we consistently underplayed the importance of mothers' work, both in the home and in the community? Are homemaking, volunteering, and part-time employment valid work options, priviledges open only to a few, or gender-assigned forms of servitude and second-class citizenship? Because of their frequent sacrifice of high salaries, career advancement, and job security, how many of us will continue to view such women as victims of male supremacy or as reactionaries who represent an inevitable but unfortunate backlash from the women's movement? Conversely, how many will see these women more as they themselves do (and as I've learned to), as part of a pivotal generation, one which has incorporated many of the strengths of the women's movement while at the same time recognizing its oversights and rejecting its weaknesses?

Notes

1. Harold L. Wilensky, "Orderly Careers and Social Participation: The Impact of Work History on Social Integration in the Middle Mass," *American Sociological Review* 26, 1961, 521–539.

2. Herbert Gans, *The Levittowners,* New York: Pantheon, 1967; August B. Hollingshead, *Elmstown Youth and Elmstown Revisited,* New York: Wiley & Sons, 1945 and 1975;

Robert S. Lynd and Helen M. Lynd, *Middletown in Transition,* New York: Harcourt Brace, 1947; John R. Seeley, R. Alexander Sim and E. W. Loosley, *Crestwood Heights,* Toronto: University of Toronto Press, 1956.

3. For a review and summary of the feminist-Marxist approach as well as a discussion of the ways traditional sociologists have looked at women, work, and family, see Natalie J. Sokoloff, *Between Money and Love: The Dialectics of Women's Home and Market Work,* New York: Praeger, 1980.

4. Carol Gilligan, *In a Different Voice: Psychological Theory and Women's Development,* Cambridge: Harvard University Press, 1982.

5. See, for example, Grace Baruch, Rosalind Barnett, and Caryl Rivers, *Lifeprints,* New York: McGraw Hill, 1982.

6. An example of this type of clinical portrait is found in Jean Baker Miller, *Toward a New Psychology of Women,* Boston: Beacon Press, 1977.

1
Understanding a Pivotal Generation: Background and Study Aims

I t is interesting to look at mothers currently in the active stages of child rearing because they represent a pivotal generation. They can neither be accurately described as "prefeminists" or "postfeminists." They are women who came of age and came to motherhood during the 1960s and 1970s, a period marked by shifting, and sometimes confusing, ideological currents and countercurrents. These currents have brought into question a number of our most basic assumptions about the importance and place of motherhood in a woman's life, the viability and strengths of the nuclear family, and about our notions of self-reliance, civic responsibility, and the belief that families and communities should take care of their own. To take into account how these shifting currents have influenced the expectations and experiences of modern mothers and how they have contributed to the development of the new synthesis, we must consider the historical context in which these individual lives have been played out.

Changing Sex Roles

Perhaps the strongest ideological current shaping the lives of contemporary women and their families has been the challenge to our assumptions about men's and women's proper roles. In the years since their childhood, modern parents have lived through the publicity surrounding the publication of Betty Freidan's *The Feminine Mystique*, the rise of the women's liberation movement, and many of the hard-won battles which have given women access to positions of status and power formerly held only by men.[1] They have also, however, lived through a period of reactionary rebuttals and rebuffs, in the form of Phyllis Schlafly and the anti-ERA campaign, Marabel Morgan's descriptions of "The Total Woman," and the continuing resistance of male-dominated institutions to open themselves to new gender-blind forms.[2] Although highly touted by numerous feminists, researchers, and policy analysts, flexible work hours, reasonably high status and well-paying part-time jobs, and the multitude of other similar arrangements which would better respond to women's needs and commitments are, at best, part of the future.

A number of the women interviewed for this research resorted to Hollywood movie imagery to place themselves and their generation in context. They drew upon movies like "Cheaper by the Dozen," with its cozy and sex-typed portrayal of motherhood with a large brood of children, to describe the neat and simplistic fantasies they once held of their future lives as wives and mothers. Yet, as adults, they see their generation portrayed in movies such as "The Turning Point," "An Unmarried Woman," and "Kramer versus Kramer," a collection of troubled individuals in conflict and searching for meaning in their lives. Over the course of this transition, roles which were once taken for granted became the subject of intense popular scrutiny; self-analysis, consciousness-raising sessions, and pop-psychologizing became vogue. As the women's movement coupled with the so-called "me" decade of the seventies, women were encouraged to view themselves not in terms of others, but as individuals in their own right.[3] One aim of this book is to examine where women in the mainstream place themselves in the midst of these changing images and how they balance their individual needs against those of their spouses and children.

Changing Images of Family Life

While many women of this pivotal generation became parents during a time when the value and rewards of mothering were in question, they now find themselves raising children in a period of renewed interest in the role of women as nurturers and family builders. Pregnant women adorn the cover of *Time* magazine, politicians extol the virtues of returning to traditional family values, and the postwar baby boom generation is settling into parenthood, civic responsibility, and middle age. The national mood supposedly has taken a conservative shift. Turning her own phrase, Freidan has written of the rising "feminist mystique," a term which expresses many women's disillusionment and discontent with the so-called "liberated" anti-family feminists of years past. In *The Second Stage*, she no longer counsels women in search of their own destinies to reject the middle-class values of home and family life (so few of them seemed willing to do so anyway), but rather, she advises them to look on the family as the fount of richness, "the nutrient of our humanness, of all our individuality."[4] After many years of ill repute, the family is once again being touted as the source of what truly matters in life.

That marriage and children can be such a source of satisfaction is hardly a shocking discovery. As we entered the 1980s, our belief in the future of the family and our nostalgia for family life was again on the upswing. If Freidan's reading of the public mood seems accurate, one can only wonder why it took her and others so long to acknowledge the value so many women have placed on motherhood and family all along.[5] In the not too distant past, it was only the rare feminist who argued for an increased appreciation of the role women play as nurturers and caregivers; attacking the family was far more popular than advocating its strengths or chances of survival.[6] Less than ten years ago, the sheer volume of critiques on the family led Alice Rossi to note "a remarkable shift has occurred...in society's opinion of the family, from a general endorsement of it as a worthwhile and stable institution to a general censure of it as an oppressive and bankrupt one whose demise is both imminent and welcome."[7]

These attacks on the family were hardly original, borrowing heavily as they did from the works of radical political philosophers and the experiences of utopian groups like the early kibbutzniks who experimented with nontraditional living styles since the first part of the century.[8] What is different, however, and what marks the generation of women under consideration here, is both the swiftness with which popular rhetoric and ideology about the family has shifted and the extent to which these shifts have become a part of our collective consciousness. In the course of less than one generation, we have moved from visions of the family as the symbol of what is good to visions of the family as the source of oppression and repression back to the family as the foundation and source of our humanness. Book titles illustrate the shifting currents and charged atmosphere in which families have been discussed, from *The Death of the Family* to *Family in Transition* to *Here to Stay*.[9] In addition to addressing the question of how women today view themselves as individuals, a second aim of this book is to examine how women see themselves as family members, how they frame their commitments and responsibilities to their husbands and children, what they give to their families, and what they expect back in return. This includes looking at how women feel about their families, and how, through their work and contributions, they are responsible for shaping the nature of family life today.

Changing Notions of Civic Responsibility

The third and final ideological current of interest concerns shifts in our notions of civic responsibility. This is a logical outgrowth of our modern emphasis on the importance of individual freedom and the consequences of membership in any social unit, even our families. In part, civic responsibility can be thought of in terms of how we frame, negotiate, and discharge the duties and responsibilities which participation in our local communities entails. There is a corollary to this conceptualization, however, which must also be addressed; that is, what do we expect back from our communities (and from our local and federal governments) in return for the time and energy we invest? Or, in Daniel Yankelovich's words, how do we define the terms of our "giving-getting compact"?[10]

Over the past decade, many critics have argued that we have become an increasingly selfish and narcissistic society. These attacks clearly have hit a sensitive nerve, and books such as Christopher Lasch's *The Culture of Narcissism* have become nationwide best sellers.[11] Some have attributed this supposed shift toward selfish preoccupations to the women's movement, with its focus on individual achievement and goals. Others have linked it to a more general societal drift in which we've come to do what we do on the basis of a strict cost accountancy in which we consider only the benefits and costs to our egocentric selves.

Most often, we think of this shift in terms of the delicate balance between individual goals and desires and the sacrifices we make for our families. Attitude surveys, for example, suggest that modern parents are less willing to sacrifice for their children (such as foregoing retirement savings to send a child to college) than parents of the pre–World War II era.[12] Another indication of changing attitudes and expectations may be found in our altered notions of what we consider a sacrifice at all. In the past, when women were defined largely in terms of mothering and family work, it was not common to think of the time mothers spent taking care of preschoolers as a sacrifice. Now, however, with mothers being wage-earners and career-conscious, there is more of a tendency to think of women who opt for full-time motherhood as making a sacrifice. By broadening our definitions of sacrifice, one can argue, we have shifted further toward the getting side of the giving–getting compact.

Shifts in the giving–getting compact also have implications for how we think about other aspects of women's roles and traditional obligations. Just as the value women place on mothering and the time they spend performing family work have been brought into question, so too have the less visible ways women have given to others, as neighbors, friends, and community volunteers. Yet in these roles as well women have contributed to their families and local communities and maintained many of the important links between families and the world at large.

But how does such unpaid family and community work fit into our current formulation of the giving–getting compact? It's difficult to say. In the early stages of the women's movement, for example, the value of the time women spent volunteering for children's organizations, churches, civic groups, and the like, was underplayed. Mothers' involvements as volunteers were discussed in less than two pages in Jesse Bernard's 350-page account of *The Future of Motherhood,* and her treatment is indicative of the way volunteering has been treated by those who viewed it as a threat to the women's movement and women's eventual attainment of equal rights.[13] Volunteer work was condemned as being exploitative of women, utilizing labor that should be monetarily rewarded. At once, it threatened to devalue the services that were provided and the service-provider. The volunteer-housewife was most susceptible to attack; she has been characterized as a woman with no other options. Volunteer work was often equated with busy work, work of little, or no, real importance. Both from the perspective of individual achievement and the advancement of women's position in the status hierarchy, it has been viewed as an impediment; the costs for women have been seen as high, the benefits low. Even recruitment campaigns for volunteers, rather than stressing a sense of giving, communality, or altruism—what the volunteer can do for others—emphasized what the volunteer could gain for herself, job skills, contacts, and so forth.

More recently, however, there has been a renewed interest in volunteer work with a shift in emphasis from self-advancement to a restatement of the importance of the local community. By revaluing and reemphasizing volunteer work, by rekindling our images of neighborhoods and communities as groups of people working together and for each other, it is prophesied that we can work our way back from the narcissistic society and, in doing so, decrease our reliance on costly public services. Once we start doing more for one another, some contend, we will start expecting less from our government, to the long-range good of us all. In short, we are witness to the renewed popularity of an old conservative line. We are being admonished to alter the terms of our giving–getting compact, to give more but expect less from our nation and our communities.

Throughout the late 1960s and 1970s, we witnessed an increase both in the number and types of government-provided services and supports to families. The metaphor of the Johnson years was "guns and butter": increases in defense spending abroad would be matched by increases in social-service programs at home. What followed were not only increases in programs directed at the poor, but a growing number of so-called social "entitlements," services not restricted by income or need. This, critics have suggested, has led to what might be termed an "entitlement mentality," the expectation that we have the right to receive goods and services whether they are critical to our welfare or not, and whether or not we give anything back in return. Many have argued that the growth of the service-sector in our society has hurt more families than it has helped, by undermining the importance of self-reliance and by relocating authority from inside the family to external sources (most notably the burgeoning number of service professionals, from social workers to family therapists and the expanding array of mental-health workers).[14] Arguments that our families are bruised, if not destroyed, by too many services are countered with powerful statistics demonstrating that too many families are still needy and require more, not fewer, supports.[15]

Debates over the pluses and minuses of the service-economy have filtered through the public as well, in political rhetoric, popular books, and media headlines. A third aim of this book is to look at these disagreements and issues from the perspective of women and their families, to examine how women in the mainstream have sorted through shifting notions of civic responsibility, how they frame the giving–getting compact with respect to their local communities, and how families draw the boundaries between their private worlds and the public world outside. To meet this aim, it is necessary to examine when families turn to services for help with the demands and stresses of child rearing; what types of supports they want and expect to receive from their communities; and perhaps most importantly, how much individuals and families are willing to give to others in return for what they take.

In sum, this is a study of the complex connections and interplay among women, families, and the community. It is an examination of women's roles in the context of how we view ourselves as members of our families and communities and as citizens who contribute to as well as partake of communal goods and services.

A Study of Adult Development

My purpose here is to consider women's lives through the lens of adult development. Instead of focusing on how females are socialized as children to develop "the sense of self as parent, the desire to be a parent, and parenting capabilities",[16] I examine how individuals assimilate new experiences and respond to life events and changing conditions in adulthood. The mothers interviewed for this research did not experience the rise of feminism during their childhood, but rather their young adult years; similarly, women did not begin returning to the labor force in large numbers until this pivotal generation reached maturity. This, then, is an examination primarily of the impact of adult experiences on the lives of adults. While it is set apart from much of the work conducted in the area of adult development in that it does not focus specifically on any one life event or transition (such as becoming a parent), it has a similar intent. It looks at how people accommodate to changes throughout adulthood, whether these changes are induced by personal events and transitions, societal-level ideological shifts, the opening up of new social roles, or economic and social conditions.

Although I do not focus on any one particular life transition, I am highlighting one identifiable stage of adulthood, the years of active parenting. Active parenting is, in many respects, one of the most constrained times of an individual's life. As studies of parenthood as well as personal narratives point out, women often become confined to their roles as wives and mothers, and men become burdened by the demands and pressures of being the primary financial provider.[17] In addition, parents in the active stages of child rearing are more likely to be tied into their neighborhoods and communities than either childless individuals or parents whose children have come of age.[18] This is, on the one hand, due to the constraints imposed by providing child care and the difficulties of traveling with youngsters and, on the other, to the fact that children, through their own activities and social contacts, anchor families to their local environments. In our interviews, when mothers were asked how their lives would be different if they didn't have children, most responded in terms of the freedoms nonparents have: without children they would be free to travel, stay out late at night, remain at work after regular hours, experiment with a new job, move to a different place, and so on. Children, by virtue of their presence and demands, impose constraints upon their parents and these constraints often lend a conservative air to men and women at this life-cycle stage. In addition, since the community shares an interest in the education and well-being of each new generation, adults are under scrutiny from the outside world while they raise their sons and daughters. Although parents hardly live in a goldfish bowl, their activities and child-rearing efforts are under the surveillance of the community at large.[19] In reading through this account of women's lives, it is helpful to bear in mind that some of the reflected conservatism may be associated with this particular life stage rather than being a stance which endures over the whole life course.

In considering women's expectations as well as the meaning they ascribe to their behavior, I draw on the work of a number of role theorists and symbolic interactionists. Such a perspective, as detailed in Berger and Luckman's *The Social Construction of Reality*[20] assumes that it is through interactions with others that individuals come to an understanding of themselves and their places in the social order. Two underlying questions posed in this research, therefore, are: How do adults come to construct and renegotiate their roles? And how do they personally interpret their actions? I am interested less here in documenting the social forces which have molded women's lives than in examining how mothers frame their commitments to others in terms of the meaning they ascribe to their maternal role and according to the understanding and expectations they have regarding what it means to be a woman in comtemporary society.

The Concept of Choice

There are few of us who would contend that women's lives are rigidly set just as few would argue that women can decide, free of constraints and encumbrances, what they would most like to do. In general, we all know that choices don't come without strings attached. Yet it is often difficult to agree on what truly constitutes a choice: When are women acting on their own and when are they following some socially defined rules over which they have little or no control?

In the following, I look at how women make decisions for themselves and their families by using a rational–decision-making model. The term "rational" used in this sense implies that individuals use appropriate means to pursue the goals they have chosen.[21] Such a model assumes that women have some degree of conscious control over the course of their lives, even though this control may be limited by their social context and social positions in society.[22] Kathleen Gerson, looking at women's decisions regarding fertility and employment, uses the concept of "structured choices."[23] This term is helpful since it at once emphasizes the availability and possibility of choice and highlights the fact that choices are limited by the social structuring of options and opportunities available of women today. The notion of structured choices is similar to the "cost-constraint" model used by Claude Fischer and his associates, as well as the framework used by exchange theorists such as Ivan Nye.[24]

Indeed, there are many variants of a basic rational–decision-making model. All assume that we can ascertain with some degree of accuracy the different alternatives which individuals have, how they weigh the advantages and disadvantages of such options, and, ultimately, what choice they choose. This does not imply, though, that people necessarily have all the information at their disposal which an objective outsider would think important for making a truly informed choice. Nor does it presuppose that individuals calculate in some mechanistic way the costs and benefits of each alternative. Instead, it assumes that women size up their situations and make decisions which seem sensible to them at the time.

For example, Kristen Luker has examined how women choose among their perceived options. Interviewing women at the time they were seeking abortions, she asked, why hadn't they prevented the unwanted pregnancy in the first place, through the use of contraceptive measures? What her work illustrates is that many women actually were informed about how to prevent an unwanted pregnancy, but chose not to use contraception anyway. This decision appears irrational until one considers the context in which the women made their decision. For many, the costs of becoming pregnant (which they viewed as a very unlikely occurrence) did not outweigh the costs of admitting their sexuality and monitoring sexual activity. For them, having intercourse without contraception seemed a sensible choice.[25] In fact, one has to remember that Luker saw only those women who actually wound up pregnant—consider those who made the same choice but did not suffer the effects of an unwanted pregnancy.

There are, however, some difficulties involved in employing a rational-decision-making model. First, it is almost impossible to get a complete answer by simply and directly asking individuals why they chose to do what they are doing. People offer partial explanations, usually either ones which seem most salient to them at the time, ones which they think will most interest the interviewer, or ones which are easiest to express. Questions must thus elicit responses along a variety of dimensions, including the many, if not overwhelming, number of factors which comprise the context in which decisions must be understood. Sometimes some of these dimensions are so taken for granted that it is difficult to remember to inquire about them. For example, when Gerson explored the question of why some women choose to have children and others don't, she at first focused on issues of employment opportunities, career aspirations, and role models. However, early in the course of interviewing, she learned that a major factor which sorted women with children from those without was the presence of a stable and enduring heterosexual relationship. Upon realizing this structural determinant of women's procreative decisions, Gerson began inquiring into the history of women's relationships with men. Only by doing so could she obtain a more complete portrait of how this choice was made.[26]

What research such as this illustrates is how critical it is to approach individuals' lives and their choices with an understanding of the context in which decisions are made. In particular, interview questions must be framed within the relevant social context. It is only within this context that we can look at women's lives and examine how the choices individual women make aggregate into social trends. Therefore, although this study is not primarily an examination of the factors which shape the context of women's lives, these factors had to be taken into account in framing the research and developing the interview materials. It was only after considering these factors that I was able to proceed to study the choices women make within the constraints of their historical setting.

In examining women's choices here, however, I don't only look at how women assess the costs and rewards of different choices for themselves. I also examine how women's assessments of the needs of others, particularly their children but their spouses as well, enter into their framing of available options. Mothers' child-rearing values influence both how women construct their maternal role and what they perceive as options available to them in other roles. Once again, women may not naturally separate what is good for them versus what is good for others. Instead, they consider their own options in terms of their personal relations and concerns for the well-being of those close to them. In other words, more often than not, a "good" job is one that not only promises personal satisfaction but one which doesn't disrupt the harmony of family life or one's intimate relations with loved ones.

A Study of Family–Community Interactions

In addition to looking at mothers as decision makers, this study is also an examination of the social structuring of family and community interactions. It relies on Ann Stueve's and my conceptualization of mothers as "social agents" for their families.[27] The concept of mothers as social agents departs from the gender-based assignments of traditional sociology. Earlier sociologists such as Talcott Parsons and Robert Bales, for example, cast fathers and not mothers as the link between the intimate world of the family and the world outside. Because of their immersion in the workplace and their access to positions of power in civic institutions, it was fathers who were seen as teaching children to perform effectively in social worlds outside the home. Mothers were portrayed as the managers within the family unit, passing on the importance of nurturance and personal relations. Research on the patterns of interactions between families and community-based institutions such as the schools, however, have forced us to revise this conceptualization, since it has brought to our attention an additional dimension of the maternal role, that of mediating between children and institutional settings. For example, Carol Joffe, in a study of early childhood programs in California, and Sara Lightfoot, in an examination of interactions between parents and teachers of school-age children, both document the extent to which mothers communicate with child-serving professionals and take charge of monitoring interactions between their family members and the institutions and professionals who serve them.[28] Due, in large part, to work-hour conflicts with school hours, fathers' participation is typically limited to special events scattered throughout the year.

As Rose Laub Coser argues, in emphasizing the nurturant and expressive functions of mothers within the family unit, we have downplayed the ways women are actively involved as mediators between their families and more formal community-based programs and activities. Reporting on her work with middle-class families, she writes that through her volunteer work in child-serving institutions, "a mother helps both to maintain the communal social network and integrate her children in it....to use Parson's phrase, she helps adapt the family to the 'external system.'"[29]

By maintaining contact with child-serving professionals, by volunteering to work in local organizations, and by participating in local neighborhoods, mothers, perhaps even more than fathers, structure their families' exposure to and involvements in social worlds outside the home. This book seeks to clarify the role women play as social agents for their families. It examines how the role of social agent is structured by mothers' employment patterns and then discusses the importance and ramifications of mothers' work as social agents for families and communities.

In conclusion, this is first and foremost a book about modern mothers. I consider not only how women's lives today are shaped by the contexts in which they live and work but also how women, in forging a new synthesis, are finding ways to realize their potential both in the home and in the wider community. By carefully considering mothers' values and actions, we can begin to appreciate the extent to which women continue to feel responsible for molding and enriching the quality of family and community life. We learn why so many mothers in the mainstream remain committed to these forms of unpaid work even at the same time they are experimenting with the rewards and benefits of employment. This deeper understanding of women's lives and priorities can ultimately contribute to the search for more equitable divisions of labor between men and women, for we are reminded that the goal is to find ways that both sexes can share not only in the world of employment but also in the unpaid family and community work which assures the vitality and survival of our society.

Notes

1. Betty Freidan, *The Feminine Mystique*, New York: Norton, 1963.

2. For a discussion of shifts in attitudes regarding feminism, see Betty Freidan, *The Second Stage*, New York: Summit Books, 1981.

3. Sheila Rothman, *Woman's Proper Place*, New York: Basic Books, 1978.

4. Betty Freidan, "Feminism's Next Step," *New York Times Magazine*, July 5, 1981, 33. See also Freidan's *The Second Stage*.

5. Joseph Featherstone makes a similar point when he ponders why so many academic doomsayers have ignored the "essential familism" of U.S., and particularly, U.S. working-class families in "Family Matters," *Harvard Educational Review* 1, February 1979, 20–53.

6. For an example of a feminist writer who has called for an increased appreciation of women's work as nurturers, see Ann Oakley's pair of books: *Becoming a Mother*, New York: Schocken, 1980; and *Women Confined: Towards a Sociology of Childbirth*, New York: Schocken Books, 1980.

7. Alice S. Rossi, "A Biosocial Perspective on Parenting," *Daedalus*, Special Issue on the Family, 1, 1977, 1.

8. See, for example, Frederick Engels, *The Origin of the Family*, 1891. In Karl Marx and Frederick Engels, *Selected Works, V. III.*, Moscow: Progress Publishers, 1970. Also Melford E. Spiro, *Kibbutz, Adventure in Utopia*, New York: Schocken Books, 1956.

9. Mary Jo Bane, *Here to Stay*, New York: Basic Books, 1976. David Cooper, *Death of the Family*, New York: Pantheon Books, 1970, and Arlene S. Skolnick and Jerome H. Skolnick, *Family in Transition*, Boston: Little, Brown and Company, 1971.

10. Daniel Yankelovich, *New Rules: Searching for Self-Fulfillment in a World Turned Upside Down*, New York: Random House, 1981.

11. Christopher Lasch, *The Culture of Narcissism*, New York: Basic Books, 1979.

12. Daniel Yankelovich, *New Rules*.

13. Jesse Bernard, *The Future of Motherhood*, New York: Penguin Books, 1974.

14. See, for examples, Christopher Lasch, *Haven in a Heartless World*, New York: Basic Books, 1977, and Jacques Donzelot, *The Policing of Families*, New York: Pantheon Books, 1979. Both authors attempt to document how government- and the public-sector, under the guise of providing services, have usurped the independence of nuclear families and weakened the power of traditional authority figures, that is, fathers.

15. Both Kenneth Keniston's *All Our Children*, New York: Harcourt, Brace, Jovanovich, 1977 and the Advisory Committee on Child Development of the National Research Council's Report, *Toward a National Policy for Children and Families*, 1979, provide statistics illustrating the need for increased services to children and their families. Joseph Featherstone's essay, "Family Matters," explains the liberal rationale behind such a call for increased government support. In contrast, however, Bergitta Berger in "The Helping Hand Strikes Again", *The Public Interest* 165, 1981, has argued that too many policy analysts and academics are victims of a liberal ideology which places a mistaken emphasis on government intervention, which ultimately hurts, rather than helps, families.

16. Nancy Chodorow, *The Reproduction of Mothering*, Berkeley: University of California Press, 1978, 90.

17. For discussion of women's confinements and constraints see Ronnie Friedland and Carol Kort, *The Mothers' Book, Shared Experiences,* Boston: Houghton Mifflin Company, 1981; Helena Lopata, *Occupation: Housewife,* New York: Oxford University Press, 1971, and Oakley, *Becoming a Mother.* For some of the constraints encountered by men, see Joseph Pleck, Graham Staines, and Linda Lang, "Work and Family Life: First Reports on Work-Family Interference and Workers' Formal Child Care Arrangements, from the 1977 Quality of Employment Survey," Working Paper No. 63, Wellesley College Center for Research on Women, 1978; and Valerie K. Oppenheimer, "The Male-Family Cycle Squeeze: The Interaction of Men's Occupational and Family Life Cycles," *Demography* 11, May 1974, 227–245.

18. Claude Fischer, R.M. Jackson, C. Ann Stueve, Kathleen Gerson, L.M. Jones, with Mark Baldassare, *Networks and Places,* New York: Free Press, 1977.

19. For a more complete discussion of how adults' lives change when they become parents, see Lydia O'Donnell, "The Social Worlds of Parents," *Marriage and Family Review* 5, Winter 1982, 9–37.

20. Peter Berger and T. Luckman, *The Social Construction of Reality,* Garden City: Doubleday, 1966.

21. This definition comes from Kristen Luker, *Taking Chances, Abortion and the Decision Not to Contracept,* Berkeley: University of California Press, 1975.

22. See, again, Natalie Sokoloff, *Between Money and Love.*

23. Kathleen Gerson, "Models of Behavior and Women's Decision-making Processes," *The New England Sociologist, Special Issue on Choice, Constraint and Change in Women's Lives,* Summer 1981.

24. Claude Fischer et al., *Networks and Places.*

25. Kristen Luker, *Taking Chances.*

26. Kathleen Gerson, "Models of Behavior and Women's Decision-making Processes."

27. This conceptualization of mothers as social agents was first detailed in Lydia O'Donnell and Ann Stueve, "Mothers as Social Agents: Structuring the Community Activities of School-Age Children," *Research in the Interweave of Social Roles, V. III,* Helena Lopata and Joseph Pleck, Eds., Greenwich: JAI Press, 1982.

28. Carol E. Joffe, *Friendly Intruders: Child Care Professionals and Family Life,* Berkeley: University of California Press, 1977; and Sara Lawrence Lightfoot, *Worlds Apart: Relationships Between Families and Schools,* New York: Basic Books, 1978.

29. Rose Laub Coser, "Authority and Structural Ambivalence in the Middle-Class Family," In R. Coser, Ed., *The Family: Its Structures and Function,* New York: St. Martins Press, 1964, 377.

2
The Study: Methods and Sample Description

During the summer and fall of 1980, two interviewers and I talked with seventy-four mothers.[1] These women were selected at random from the town census lists of two communities in the Boston metropolitan area. The first, Claremont, houses a largely white working- and lower-middle-class population; the second, Green Haven, is a more affluent suburb and most of its residents are middle and upper-middle class.[2] The women who talked with us shared one characteristic in common: they all had at least one child twelve years of age or younger.

In order to obtain this sample of mothers, letters explaining the purposes of the study and what participation would entail were sent to the randomly drawn names of women residents in each community who were between the ages of twenty and forty-nine. All the women were then contacted by phone and of those who were eligible for the study (that is, who had a child of the right age), 78 percent agreed to participate in the research. As evidenced by this fairly high proportion of positive responses, most of the women contacted were eager for the opportunity to recount their experiences and to express their ideas and values regarding child rearing and the importance of family life.

Over the course of the interviews, which lasted anywhere from two to five hours, the women were asked to provide information not only on their own schedules and activities, but also on the activities and progress of their children, and on the family, employment, and community involvements of their spouses. It would have been preferable, if time and financial constraints were not a factor, to interview children and husbands separately about their own experiences. However, as I learned in previous research, insistence on interviews with more than one member of a given family not only dramatically increases the costs of research but, perhaps more critically, it considerably lowers the percentage of families who agree to participate, thus affecting the validity of the sample. In addition, by comparing interviews from wives with those from husbands, this prior research suggests that women can be used as fairly reliable sources about the everyday activities of their family members.[3]

The mothers who agreed to be interviewed were asked to answer a number of questions regarding: the early years of their marriage, the events surrounding the birth of their children, and their family and child-rearing involvements leading up to the present; their employment histories, career plans and aspirations; their current activities and commitments, including employment, child-care arrangements, and community volunteer-work; their patterns of interaction and exchange with family, friends, co-workers, and neighbors; their past and current usage of community-based services for families and the level and quality of their interactions with those professionals who provide services; their values and attitudes regarding child rearing, family life, women's employment, and community participation; their children's activities and social involvements; and their husbands' work schedules, child-rearing contributions, and community activities. In addition, basic demographic and social information was obtained as well as information on the respondents' family backgrounds and accounts of their own mothers' employment histories and child-rearing arrangements. In general, an effort was made to obtain the same basic information from each respondent. However, the women were also encouraged to talk at length on topics which interested them and had particular relevance to their own lives. Many did so, and the interviews, on the whole, lasted far longer than was originally anticipated. With permission, these interviews were tape-recorded for later analysis.

Study Design

As with any kind of endeavor, I was forced to make a number of choices to set reasonable limitations on the scope of this research. These decisions determined the number of women contacted; the type and depth of information collected from each respondent; and the nature of the interview situation itself. Within the limitations of available resources, I sought to obtain as much information as I could about women's lives and commitments.

The study itself lies somewhere between ethnographies, which record a wealth of information on the lives of a few individuals who are assumed to typify a given culture or ethnic subgroup, and broad-scale survey research, which records a limited amount of information on a relatively large, and hopefully representative, population. On the one hand, I do not have enough material and information on each subject's life to provide an ethnographic account; the following does not, therefore, contain the detailed case studies which are common in such reports. On the other hand, I did not need to force women to choose among a limited number of close-ended responses to a limited number of preset questions; I neither had to restrict severely the interview interactions nor the types of information I set out to obtain. Through the use of many questions, I cast a wide net: I wanted to learn about a great many aspects of women's lives and I wanted to know about each of these aspects in some detail. While not an ethnography (primarily since we did not have the resources to conduct prolonged observations of family life), the interviews allowed enough room for discussion so that we are able to gain a perspective on how mothers view their lives and how they interpret their experiences. Because of this detail, however, it was necessary to limit the number of women interviewed. In short, there is always a tradeoff between the type of information desired and the sample size. We did not contact enough subjects to claim that findings, in and of themselves, can be generalized to draw conclusions about the lives of all mothers nationwide. The sample was drawn carefully enough, however (and there was a high enough response rate), so that it is possible to identify and piece together various themes which run through the interviews and begin to sort out differences and similarities in how mainstream women experience motherhood.

Analysis

As I think will be amply illustrated in the text, the interviews yielded the desired information—and then some. Many, many details were collected on the lives of each of the seventy-four women who talked with us. This sheer quantity of information posed some problems, since the data had to be reduced to a manageable level. Parts of this data reduction were easy. Basic demographic information, such as the ages of respondents and their children, was quickly and easily coded, directly from the notes interviewers made while women were answering questions.

The rest of the interview material was more difficult to deal with and took far longer to sort through. To preserve the integrity and richness of women's responses, and to be able to analyze the data thematically, it was necessary to transcribe the bulk of the interview sessions. This was a cumbersome, costly, and time-consuming task. A typical interview took almost eight hours to transcribe and resulted in anywhere from fifteen to forty single-spaced typed pages of material. Needless to say, this resulted in a massive amount of paperwork; there were over twenty-five hundred pages of interview data from just this relatively small group of respondents. Simply to wade through the resulting stack of paper was an effort; reducing the data so that it could be analyzed was a painstaking job. First, a code book, with specific measures for most of the topics under consideration, was developed. This code book included quantifiable material and counts on a range of topics, from how long women had been married and how old they were when they became mothers, to statistics on their employment histories, current schedules, and measures of both husbands' and wives' volunteer work and level of involvement in their neighborhoods and communities. Specific codes and measures will be discussed in more detail in subsequent chapters, as the need arises, along with the frequencies, distributions, and cross-tabulations of relevant variables.

In addition to the considerable amount of data which was readily codified, there were mounds of additional information which lent themselves only to more thematic or qualitative anlysis. It was necessary to conserve much of this material to retain the ways in which women discussed their lives and the words they used to describe their multiple obligations. Pages of transcription were, therefore, grouped by topic; all the material having to do with women's feelings about employment, for example, were placed together. After multiple readings through the material on each topic, similar phrases, issues, and themes were identified and those parts of the transcriptions which dealt with similar ideas were placed together. Through these efforts, it is possible to present not only second-hand interpretations and analysis but also actual, and at times lengthy, quotations from women which speak to relevant issues and themes. While the responsibility for sifting and sorting through data and picking out cogent issues remains with the researcher, this type of study and this type of analysis hopefully also allows us to hear women speak for themselves.

In the remainder of this chapter, I describe the women and the communities in which they live in greater detail. Subsequent chapters then focus on women's commitments to child rearing, employment, and community involvement.

The Sample

The Communities: Claremont

The first community, Claremont, was chosen for study because of its predominately white working- and lower–middle-class population and its well established and diverse service sector. With almost 55,000 residents, Claremont is at the end of one of the major trolley lines running into Boston; it also has a reliable municipal bus service with routes through the center of town. Within its borders, there are a number of quite affluent and desireable areas, particularly around the lake front, which house wealthy businessmen and professionals. For the most part, however, Claremont is home to a large number of blue-collar workers, municipal employees, and local proprietors. Claremont is readily accessible from downtown Boston and contains a variety of moderately priced and affordable places to live, including small single-family houses, duplexes, apartments, and even a federally subsidized housing project open to veterans and their families.

Like many New England towns, Claremont is heavily Catholic. In the local newspaper, apartments and two-family houses offered for rent are often listed by the parish in which they are located. In the center of town is the oldest, largest, and according to many Catholic residents, most conservative church, St. Theresa's. St. Theresa's serves many of the older residents who live close by; the number of funerals held in its chapel by far surpasses the number of marriages and christenings. More recently constructed and more progressive Catholic churches are located throughout the town and tend to draw younger congregants, including those who reside in the more affluent suburbs which border Claremont on the west and north. In addition to these Catholic churches, there are a variety of other places of worship, representing most of the Protestant denominations. All in all, there are over twenty-five churches within Claremont; driving through town, one is rarely out of sight of a church steeple. Claremont is also heavily ethnic. Although most of the women interviewed were at least the second (if not the third or fourth) generation of their families to be born in this country, a majority still think of themselves as Irish-, Italian-, Greek-, or Armenian–Americans. There are only a handful of black residents, many of whom are affiliated with Boston's large academic community.

The size of a small city, Claremont is a community with a wide variety of services and organizations. The civic leaders we spoke with to learn more about the town and its facilities expressed pride in their community and, in particular, its array of children's services. Despite being plagued by some typically "modern" problems, such as an increase in vandalism at the public schools, the service-providers generally gave an impression that things run smoothly. Local personnel are well informed and have been successful at obtaining federal and state support for many diverse programs, including a number of demonstration projects at both the elementary and high school levels. (Some of these programs, however, have been recently threatened by cuts in federal spending and by the institution of Proposition 2½, which substantially cut and set limits on local taxes.) Over the years, several private benefactors have bequeathed trusts to pet charities which still provide the foundations for current fund-raising efforts. Scouting programs and the local Boys Club rely on these endowments. Town money is available to augment public and private resources and is allocated both to fill unavoidable gaps and to expand community-based recreational facilities.

Reflecting its size and the needs of its residents, Claremont provides services to both the general public and more specially identified groups. The town Recreation Department, for example, runs many services, including after-school enrichment programs which are open to all community children and summer camp and weekend activities for young residents with special needs. Low-income preschoolers are served by a local Headstart, and a network of private nursery schools and day-care centers provide a variety of curricula approaches at a range of prices. In addition, through federal and state support, Claremont has a number of programs geared to deal with the problems of troubled youth, the unemployed, alcoholics and their families, housing-project residents, the elderly, the widowed, and so on. Churches and other private groups also sponsor diverse activities: youth groups, senior citizen's clubs, sports teams, and the like.

The Communities: Green Haven

In contrast to Claremont, Green Haven is a relatively small (population approximately 29,000) and homogeneous white middle- and upper-middle-class community. It is one of the more prestigious suburbs in the Boston area; the majority of residents earn well over the national median income for married white couples.[4] Although Green Haven is home to only about half the number of people who live in Claremont, in area the two communities are about the same size. Green Haven is thus more sprawling and contains only a handful of multifamily residences, most notably a number of recently built condominiums. Younger families, in particular, have to be quite well off to live in Green Haven; rising housing prices and mortgage interest rates have made it difficult for even upper middle-income families to purchase a home. Many doctors, lawyers, engineers, and businessmen make Green Haven their home.

The residents of Green Haven are very dependent upon their cars. There is little public transportation either within the town or into the city. In contrast to Claremont, where a number of fathers and the majority of employed mothers are likely to be working within town limits, practically all workers in Green Haven have to commute back and forth to work, some to Boston, some to the Route 128 high tech industries, and some to regional shopping malls. Children, too, are more often reliant on private transportation and need to be chauffeured to their friends' houses and to after-school activities and lessons. While in Claremont, hockey and football are the favored sports of both children and parents, in Green Haven these sports are out of vogue. Instead, children participate in the town's rapidly growing and competitively successful soccer program and take lessons in gymnastics, swimming, tennis, and dance.

If in Claremont one is struck by the number of churches, the most conspicuous buildings in Green Haven are schools. The high school, in particular, is set near the middle of the town's one shopping area and has a large and well-manicured lawn leading up to its front stairs. Whereas Claremont has a commercial area which stretches from one end of town to the other, the shopping area in Green Haven is confined to the town center and two intersecting roads, Main Street and Central Road. Only a few blocks from the center of town, both streets become residential. In these residential areas, a landscape of private homes is broken up only by an occasional elementary-school building.

Practically all of the services offered within Green Haven are directed at children. The town maintains a large swimming area on its lake which is always crowded in the summer. The local YMCA offers programs for children from infancy through adolescence, including a popular summer camp. The public schools sponsor a variety of after-school activities and a regional girl-scout camp is located on the outskirts of town. In addition, there are many private children's programs: camps, music and dance centers, and so on. There are, however, no full-day child-care centers, even though the number of nursery schools has more than doubled over the past decade. Unlike Claremont, there are no local teenage drop-in centers, no unemployment offices, and few special programs geared to needy residents. Although both communities have a substantial percentage of elderly residents, Green Haven is far behind Claremont in the number and variety of programs it offers to senior citizens.

Claremont and Green Haven are thus different in a number of important ways. On the whole, residents of Claremont are less educated, with an average of 12.5 years of education per resident versus the 13.4 years of Green Haven men and women. They are also less affluent, with a median household income which is approximately 75 percent of that in Green Haven. Whereas in Green Haven most families earn more than the national median income for white couples, in Claremont most earn at or below this level. In addition, the population of Claremont is more diverse; aside from nuclear families, the town houses a substantial number of single people, students, the elderly, and single-parent households. In contrast, Green Haven is more a place where couples go to raise children. Finally, while Claremont offers a wide range of services for the general public, the young, the old, and the low-income, services and programs in Green Haven reflect its more homogeneous nature, and are far more limited in scope and in clientele. Taken together, these two communities provide a good starting place for choosing a sample of mainstream mothers to talk with about family and community life.

The Women

Thirty-eight of the women interviewed lived in Claremont and thirty-six lived in Green Haven. One of the primary reasons for drawing a sample from both these communities was to gain access to the variety of familes in what we think of as "the middle," or the mainstream, of U.S. life. Although Claremont can be thought of as a working- and lower-middle-class town, its residents have considerably more resources and opportunities than the financially strapped working-class poor who are described in Lillian Rubin's *Worlds of Pain*. [5] Similarly, while families in Green Haven are for the most part affluent, they are neither independently wealthy nor among the real elite. On a broad scale, then, the women and their families in the two communities are similar; neither rich nor poor, they can all best be thought of as being in the middle. Yet within this rather large and amorphous middle, there are differences which are important both in terms of the ways individuals interpret their lives and structure their days and in terms of the ways families are involved in their communities. This section describes the basic similarities and differences between women respondents who lived in Claremont and those who lived in Green Haven. (See table 2–1 at the end of the chapter for the demographic characteristics of the women and their families by town.)

With regard to both age and stage in the family cycle, the respondents from both communities were very much alike. The majority of mothers were in their mid- to late thirties (59 percent); only three out of the total sample of seventy-four were twenty-nine years of age or younger. In Green Haven, the median age of respondents was 36.1 years; in Claremont, it was 37.9. In both towns, approximately 35 percent of the women had at least one child under six years of age, while in the remaining 65 percent of the families, the youngest child was between the ages of six and twelve.

In a number of other ways, however, the residents of Claremont and Green Haven differed, reflecting the socio-economic characteristics of the communities in which they live. In Claremont, almost two-thirds of the women had no more than high-school educations; in Green Haven, by contrast, 65 percent were at least college graduates and many of these women had earned masters' degrees as well. In addition to this range in educational levels, there was also a spread of family incomes. In Claremont, the majority of families earned around or under the median income for families in the Boston metropolitan area. Thirty-four percent lived on less than $20,000 a year; only one family had an income of $40,000 a year or more. In Green Haven, not one family reported an income of less than $20,000, while almost 40 percent earned over $40,000 (although usually just slightly over).

Families in Green Haven had higher incomes despite the fact that they were more likely to be reliant on only one salary. At the time of their interviews, 50 percent of the mothers in this community were full-time homemakers as compared to only 32 percent of the women in Claremont. Simply stated, more women in Green Haven could afford to be at home. Whereas close to 70 percent of the women in Claremont had taken a paid job by the time their youngest child was five, only one-half of the mothers in Green Haven had been employed at the same time they were raising a preschooler. (Even this lower percentage, however, is testimony to the dramatic increase in the number of mothers with young children to enter the labor force.) The overall employment rate of 58 percent among women in both communities is similar to nationwide data which indicated that just over 50 percent of all white mothers with children under eighteen were employed during the year this study was conducted. Despite the fact that almost three-fifths of the women were employed, only 16 percent contributed more than $10,000 a year to their family incomes. One reason for these low earnings, which reflect the wages typically earned by mothers[6], is that many of the employed women worked part-time or for only part of the year, arrangements which will be discussed in more detail in a later chapter.

Husbands' occupations can also be used as an indicator of the social-class distinctions between Claremont and Green Haven. Twice as many fathers in Green Haven held jobs at the professional or technical levels (53 percent as opposed to 26 percent). An additional 30 percent of the men in Green Haven were mid- to upper-level managers and administrators, as opposed to 18 percent of the fathers in Claremont. In Claremont, approximately one-quarter of the men held jobs as municipal blue-collar employees, tradesmen, and service workers; only one man in Green Haven was so employed, and his family was the most income-restricted of all interviewed in that town.

While the vast majority of women were married at the time they were interviewed, seven (18 percent) of the women in Claremont were either divorced or separated from their husbands. Only one woman in Green Haven was living apart from her spouse and she questioned whether she would be able to keep up with housing costs and living expenses now that she was on her own. Approximately 10 percent of the women in both communities had been married more than once.

The residents of Green Haven lived in private houses and all but a handful owned their own homes. While a few of these houses were relatively small (a fact which distressed their inhabitants), for the most part living quarters were spacious, well-furnished, and offered a considerable amount of privacy to each family member. Fifty-three percent of the women in Green Haven had two children; only 36 percent had three or more. In contrast, not only did more of the women in Claremont have larger families (with 53 percent having three or more children), but more of the women—particularly those who were divorced—had only one child (24 percent compared to 11 percent in Green Haven). The living arrangements of Claremont residents were also more diverse. While a handful of women lived in houses similar to those in the more wealthy suburb, homes in Claremont were generally smaller and older. Some Claremont mothers lived in rented two-bedroom apartments or duplexes; a few shared mother–daughter type houses with their own parents. Privacy, more difficult to come by in larger families and smaller living spaces, seemed to be less stressed in Claremont. While in both communities interviews at times took place in the presence of preschoolers, older children in Green Haven, when they were home, were usually asked to retire to their rooms or play outside while their mothers talked. It was more often in Claremont that youngsters listened in on the interview, adding their own comments when a particular question caught their interest.

Almost half the women interviewed were Catholic; Claremont women, however, were more likely to be Catholics. An additional difference is that there were no Jews among the Claremont women, while 22 percent of the Green Haven women were Jewish. These Jewish women were among the most highly educated mothers in the sample.

Finally, residents of Claremont were likely to have spent more years living in their communities; some, in fact, still lived in the same neighborhoods in which they grew up. Over 50 percent of the women in Claremont had lived there for more than ten years, while only 22 percent of the women in Green Haven were such long-term residents. Because of their proximity, grandparents and other relatives were more readily available to women in Claremont. Not only had the Claremont mothers themselves not moved away, but their relations were also less likely to move, whether to take a new job or to retire to Florida. By contrast, mothers in Green Haven were more mobile. After going to college, many of them had lived in several locations around the country before coming or, more often, before returning to the Boston area. Frequently, these moves were predicated upon their husbands' training and job promotions. These differences in mobility patterns were played out in the ways the women thought about their neighborhoods and communities. Almost twice as many residents of Claremont said they knew their neighbors and saw them often. In Claremont, having your mother "close by" meant she lived in the same neighborhood or town; in Green Haven, "close by" more often meant she lived in the same state.

In short, there are enough similarities among the women and their families in Green Haven and Claremont for the residents of both communities to fit into our notion of families "in the middle." There are also sufficient differences, however, to give us insights into the factors which shape different patterns of mothering, family life, and community participation, and to provide us with a portrait which illustrates some of the diversity of life in two mainstream U.S. communities.

How Representative Are the Women and Their Communities?

In any study, consideration must be given to whether the conclusions which are drawn are valid and to what extent findings can be generalized to a broader population. This is especially true when the sample size is relatively small and has been gathered from a geographically limited area, as is the case here.

On the one hand, it is clear that Claremont and Green Haven have many characteristics which make them typical of the types of communities in which working- and middle-class families raise their children. According to census reports, the majority of families across the country live in similar towns.[7] Their size, proximity to an urban center, residential character, as well as the social-class compositions of their populations make them good candidates as "typical" suburbs of the United States. However, as always, there were some disadvantages to choosing these particular study sites, some characteristics of the communities which make them deviate from the abstract notion of typical and take on a character of their own. For example, reflecting the demographic characteristics of New England in general, both towns have Catholic populations which are relatively larger than the national norm. The percentage of residents who

Table 2-1
Selected Demographic Information on the Women and Their Families by Town

	Total Sample	Claremont	Green Haven
Number of Respondents	74	38	36
Median Age	37 years	37.9 years	36.1 years
Family Stage			
Youngest Child under 6 Years	35% (26)	34% (13)	36% (13)
Youngest Child 6–12 Years	65% (48)	66% (25)	64% (23)
Educational Attainment[a]			
High School/Less	37% (27)	58% (22)	14% (5)
Some College or Technical School	20% (15)	18% (7)	22% (8)
College Graduate	43% (32)	24% (9)	64% (23)
Family Income[a,b]			
Under $20,000/Year	18% (13)	34% (13)	0 (0)
$20,000–$29,999	35% (26)	40% (15)	31% (11)
$30,000–$39,999	24% (18)	21% (8)	28% (10)
Over $40,000	20% (15)	3% (1)	39% (14)
Employment Status			
At Home	42% (31)	32% (12)	50% (18)
Part-time Employed	42% (31)	52% (20)	33% (12)
Full-time Employed	16% (12)	16% (6)	17% (6)
Marital Status			
Married	89% (66)	82% (31)	97% (35)
Not married	11% (8)	18% (7)	3% (1)
Number of Children			
One	18% (13)	24% (9)	11% (4)
Two	38% (28)	24% (9)	53% (19)
Three	23% (17)	32% (12)	14% (5)
Four or More	22% (16)	21% (8)	22% (8)
Religion			
Catholic	49% (36)	55% (21)	42% (15)
Protestant	26% (19)	26% (10)	25% (9)
Jewish	11% (8)	0 (0)	22% (8)
NA	15% (11)	18% (7)	11% (4)
Length of Residence[a]			
10 years or less	61% (45)	47% (18)	75% (27)
Over 10 years	39% (29)	53% (20)	25% (9)

[a]Differences between towns are significant at least at the .05 level
[b]Missing data = 2 on income.

identify with an ethnic group is also higher than one might encounter in some midwestern suburb. Probably as a result of these factors, there were lower rates of divorce and remarriage among respondents than are the current national average. To some degree, these factors shaped how women responded to questions. It is possible, therefore, that the women interviewed for the purposes of this study are somewhat more conservative than other mothers in different locales. It is perhaps equally possible, however, given the location of the study in the Northeast and the sizable academic and liberal community in the Boston metropolitan area, that the women are more liberal than their counterparts elsewhere. It becomes critical, then, to compare the experiences of respondents and their social contexts with accounts of women residing in similar communities across the country. Doing so, I think there is evidence that while this research is based on interviews with one group of women in one particular area, we would find more similarities than differences between the mothers described here and other mainstream women. First, the labor force participation rates, employment patterns, and child-bearing and child-rearing decisions of the women are typical of those of other white mothers from similar class backgrounds.[8] Second, the women's accounts of the stresses and rewards of mothering and the types of work and family arrangements they prefer strike a familiar note with other studies.

One illustration of such similarities can be found in research conducted by Lynne McCallister. Interviewing sixty-four women residing in what she termed "middle-American neighborhoods" in the California area, McCallister reports almost identical work and family arrangements. The women she spoke with expressed their commitments to the maternal role in similar terms. As she summarized in her research, "These mothers preferred a balanced work pattern, combining mothering and other household work with gradually increasing amounts of public work as their children grew older, believing they gave their children something no one else could provide, and also wanting the experience of mothering for themselves."[9] Such findings are mutually supportive; taken together with national statistics, there is no doubt but that they bolster the conclusions and arguments presented here.

Notes

1. These interviews were part of a larger study of families and care-giving funded under a National Science Foundation grant to the Wellesley College Center for Research on Women; Laura Lein was principal investigator. The two interviewers who joined me in talking with mothers were Christina Pershing and Diana Taylor, research interviewers at the Wellesley Center.

2. The socio-economic characteristics of each community were obtained from the U.S. Bureau of the Census, Census of Population: 1979. General Social and Economic

Characteristics Final Report PC (1)-D23 Massachusetts. Washington: U.S. General Printing Office, 1972.

3. This previous research was The Families and Communities Project, funded by the National Institute of Mental Health; the principal investigator was Laura Lein. As part of this study, approximately forty couples were interviewed. When interviews from husbands and wives were compared, accounts of daily events and the household division of labor and child care were found to be quite similar. Because insistence on having both husbands and wives participate in the research was causing the majority of families to refuse and greatly increasing sampling costs, an additional set of interviews was then conducted with wives only.

4. In Claremont, 74 percent of respondents had household incomes of less than $30,000 a year while in Green Haven 67 percent had over this amount. The national income for all married couples was between $22,400 and $27,740 (depending on whether wives were employed) around the time of the study. Given that respondents were all white and resided in the relatively expensive metropolitan Boston area, their incomes were expectedly somewhat higher, but still within the ballpark of what we consider middle-income. See Howard Hayghe, "Dual Earner Families," Joan Aldous, Ed., *Two Paychecks: Life in Dual Earner Families,* Beverly Hills: Sage, 1982.

5. Lillian Rubin, *Worlds of Pain: Life in the Working-Class Family,* New York: Basic Books, 1969.

6. For statistics on maternal employment see Allyson S. Grossman, "Working Mothers and their Children," *Monthly Labor Review* 104, 5, 1981, 49–54; Beverly L. Johnson and Elizabeth Waldman, "Marital and Family Patterns of the Labor Force," *Monthly Labor Review* 104, 10, 1981, 36–38; and George Masnick and Mary Jo Bane, *The Nation's Families: 1960-1990,* Boston: Auburn House, 1982.

7. Mary Jo Bane, *Here to Stay.*

8. See Mary Jo Bane and George Masnick, *The Nation's Families* as well as Joan Aldous, Ed., *Two Paychecks: Life in Dual Earner Families.*

9. Lynne Sherwin McCallister, "Planning for Mothers' Work: Jobs, Child Care and Homemaking in Four Middle American Neighborhoods," Doctoral Dissertation submitted to the University of California, Berkeley, 1982, 2.

Part II
Placing Themselves in Context: Women Recall Their Pasts

3
Expectations of Motherhood

We each carry with us a personal history, an account not only of when particular transitions and events have occurred in our own lives— our school graduations, when we moved away from home, the timing of our marriages, the births of our children—but also a broader sense of where we are placed in the context of history, in the flow of changing circumstances and ideas which characterize successive generations. By constructing our historical pasts, we gain the opportunity to look at our present lives and our expectations of the future in counterpoint to our understanding of from whence we've come. Accordingly, as a way of explaining their current lives, early in their interviews, women presented their personal histories. They recounted not only the details and specific events of their pasts, as they were asked to do, but they also took pains to place themselves in terms of historical time, and particularly, in juxtaposition to those shifting ideologies dictating women's roles as wives and mothers and as individuals and achievers outside the family circle. Using the cultural stereotypes, images, and plans of their youth as a frame of reference, the women could best talk of their present lives and commitments with respect to how much they have followed or departed from the expectations and norms of their pasts.

Self-reflections

One couldn't expect to go into someone's home and ask questions on any subject and be met with a high level of self-awareness and reflection. Yet the subject of mothering and women's roles is central to the lives of the individuals who were interviewed.[1] Most had discussed what we think of as women's issues many times before, with their husbands, friends, and in some cases, their children. In fact, many see themselves as historians; they feel they have been privy to dramatic shifts in our understanding of what it means to be a woman and mother. Each woman knows other women who have taken different paths, who have made different decisions and compromises. As Karl Mannheim observed, it is in the "course of this collision with other possible forms of existence that our own mode of life becomes apparent to us."[2] For the women described here, there have been many such collisions, and a good part of their lives and activities have thus been brought into conscious consideration. This degree of self-reflection and the extent to which the women appear to examine their lives in terms of changing ideologies reflects their position as a pivotal generation and is a testament to the influence of the women's movement and its questioning of women's position in society.

Regardless of whether the women think of themselves as traditional and conservative or as liberal and open to new ways, they shared one common perception—that women's options have expanded and that there is today a freedom and openness which was not available in the days when they were young. Perhaps the most dominant theme which emerged from the interviews is just this: the presumption of how much things have changed. It is possible to report statistics on women's low salaries and confinement to the lower rungs of occupational success and conclude that not much has changed at all. This is not how the world looks to the women here, however, for in the context of personal lives and ambitions, the changes do indeed seem dramatic. Many more options now seem available, and the range of acceptable behaviors also seems far greater, from living with a man before marriage to delaying marriage and child bearing in order to pursue personal goals. It is not odd, then, that the women—most of whom are just entering into midlife—made it sound like they were young during some distant time long, long ago. Their interviews are riddled with phrases such as "way back in my generation," "that's the way it was then," "you have to understand we looked at things differently then," and "things were so different then." Thirty-year-old women as well as women in their midforties spoke of their pasts in similar terms.

In part, this aura of change and the perception that so much time has passed can be dismissed as an artifact, created by our national obsession with youth and the tendency of media to portray women past their twenties as over the hill. In part, too, it can be viewed as an expression of our natural tendency to reify and oversimplify the past. However, in the process of such reminiscing, we usually romanticize and glorify bygone days. This was not the case here. If anything, the old rules and norms for women's behavior were presented too bleakly and starkly, as if there were no room for exceptions. For example, 40 percent ($n=30$) of the women had mothers who were employed at the time the respondents were children. Yet most envision their childhood as a time when all mothers were full-time homemakers. Somehow hindsight tends to create a somewhat artificial past which can seem quite removed from the complexities and subtleties of the present.

There is a further reason for the distinctions women draw between their accounts of the present and the past, however, that may have more to do with the interview situation itself. The interviews presented women with the opportunity to distance themselves, to view their lives with a certain degree of objectivity. Women were encouraged to talk about their lives as a totality; they were neither constrained to follow a rigid protocol nor forced to answer questions in terms of preset categories. This openness and informality was essential. Following the lead of such eminent and successful interviewers as Studs Terkel, the interview format gave women the opportunity to discover what they think. By contrasting their reflections of the past with their interpretations of the present, they were able to explore and relate, in the words of Mannheim, "the inner connections between their roles, their motivations, and their own manner and type of experiencing the world."[3] Probing questions were usually not necessary; most of the women felt they had a story to tell and a type of lifestyle to portray and were grateful for an audience willing to listen. In the midst of so much popular discussion of what women should do and what different groups of women are doing, they wanted their own choices and opinions to be heard. That is why they agreed to participate in the research and that is why, in so many cases, they went on talking long after the originally agreed upon two hours were over. In other words, the interview presented women with the opportunity to reflect on who they are and how they got there.

In recounting their early lives, then, the women tended to interweave accounts of the past with their present understandings and perceptions. There is always a danger of using this type of retrospective data in inappropriate ways, to forget that our memories become distorted by our current perceptions. Yet my primary interest in this section is not to recreate the past with any degree of objective reliability, but to see how individuals draw upon their histories in order to understand their present lives. In the remainder of this chapter, I attempt to unravel these intricate weavings of past and present to start exploring how the women view the progression of their lives—where they have come from, how they perceive society has changed in their lifetime, and how they have adjusted their own values and understandings to accommodate these changes. More specifically, I look both at women's expectations about being mothers and at how family events such as marriage and the birth of children have fit into their lives. In the next chapter, I then turn to women's expectations about the place of employment and the importance of a career. These descriptions will set the stage for subsequent chapters which focus more directly on women's behaviors and their actual family, work, and community responsibilities.

Motherhood: The Social Convention

All but one of the women had expected that they would one day become mothers. This, in itself, is hardly surprising. After all, we did not set out to talk with women who have remained childless; if we had, perhaps we would have found that their expectations were different. Finding a few exceptions, however, would not discount how ingrained the expectation of motherhood is for most women, now or in the past. As a number of studies report, eighteen and nineteen-year olds in the late 1970s, just like their counterparts who were questioned nearly fifty years ago, share similar expectations that they will one day bear children.[4]

Despite this similarity, respondents made one distinction between their own experience and that of the present generation. They feel that becoming a mother, for them, was more a matter of allegiance to social convention and less a matter of conscious choice than they believe it is for young women today. Looking back on their own childhoods, they protrayed motherhood as so taken for granted that it was hardly a life transition that required much thought or careful consideration. As a result, one simply didn't concern oneself with mulling over the difficulties of being a mother or considering any of the sacrifices which motherhood might entail. As Maria O'Malley, a thirty-eight-year-old mother of two, recounted:

> I never thought there were any problems involved. I never thought it was work. I just never thought about it. . . it was just sort of an accepted thing to be a mother. You didn't think about it, you just did it! There was no choice involved. . . . I was going to do it, period. . . . That sounds a little strange, now—but that's the way it was then.

Many others, both younger and older, echoed her sentiments: "there was never any doubt that I would be a mother," "I never made any judgment of whether motherhood was going to be good or bad, it was just going to be. I never thought, 'oh, I just can't wait to have it happen because it's going to be so wonderful.' I just never thought about it," "Everyone grew up and got married and I wanted to do that and I don't think I ever really thought beyond marriage and having children and aren't they cute." Or, finally, as one woman succinctly put it, "I'm of a generation where you didn't figure things out."

At most, as youngsters, the women constructed fantasies of being the perfect mother with perfectly behaved children. As Nancy Shine, a forty-one-year-old mother of three, explained:

> Oh, gee—I always fantasized about it. . . . That's why I think I get so disappointed when now they don't do the things that I think they should do. I just can't believe they're not the perfect creatures that I was going to have. It was just going to be happy ever after and everything was going to be perfect because that's the way I wanted it. I was going to have *the* kids; they were going to be the best. They would never swear or do anything wrong. It was going to be easy.

With the exception of those who spun similar fantasies of how easy and perfect everything would be, most women had looked upon motherhood deterministically, as an event which was bound to occur at some point in their lives—after all, didn't it happen to everyone? In response to questions regarding their expectations about mothering and whether they planned on combining employment with child rearing, many simply replied, "I never really thought about it at all."

How much greater thought and consideration young women devote to the topic of motherhood today and how much more leeway there is for choosing whether one wants to be a parent, whether there really is some difference, is open to question. A perception of change is not the same as change itself. While schools offer a growing number of courses in parenting, the ability to plan for the future, as anyone who has lived or worked with adolescents comes to realize, is not a strength of the young. The perception of a difference between their pasts and current times may have more to do with the respondents' aging than with changes in the ways young girls today perceive their options. This was pointed out by several women who bemoaned their own youthful lack of foresight but also wondered, "Do teenagers ever really think about such things—do you think about any of the problems when you are young?"

One additional reason to doubt how much change has really occurred is the fact that to become a parent is still to follow social conventions: expectations of motherhood are usually born out in reality. As demographers report, the vast majority of women continue to opt for motherhood.[5] In the final analysis, being a mother still has many attractions; it continues to occupy large portions of the fantasy lives of young girls.[6] As Lisa Carr, a housewife who has plans to return to work when her youngest child enters first grade, reported:

> My ten-year-old daughter is really into it at this point, being a mother and having children. That's all she talks about. You'd think in this day of being liberated she'd be different. I've given her all these choices—many more than I've ever had—of what she can do and I tell her being a mother isn't everything. But it doesn't make any difference to her. She's the most unliberated child I've ever met. All she wants to do is get pregnant and have babies.

Sex-role theorists suggest that Mrs. Carr may only be describing an inevitable stage young girls pass through in their development as women.[7] However, there is no denying that such sentiments are still rewarded and condoned. In spite of her expressed reservations about her daughter's seeming rejection of "liberation" Mrs. Carr was quite obviously proud of her offspring's feelings of nurturance and her desire to copy what she sees her own mother doing every day. Indeed, it is the rare parent who wishes a daughter (or, for that matter, a son) to remain childless. Mrs. Carr placed a high priority on being a mother at this point in her life and it is in her capacity as a mother that she remains most visible and available to her children. It thus follows that her daughter advocates motherhood.

The pressures and incentives to become a mother continue to be quite strong. For many women, these overcome the choice supposedly afforded by the availability of contraception and by the nominal acceptance of the notion that women can do other things with their lives. Interestingly, only one woman interviewed reported having any difficulty deciding whether she wanted a child. Not only was this woman atypical in that she was one of the most highly educated and career-oriented mothers, with a master's degree and thoughts of returning to school for a doctorate, but she also has an older sister who decided to remain childless and is now a successful college professor. In the way she remembered her deliberations over whether to become a mother, this woman calls to mind media portrayals of similar high-powered career women who carefully weigh the costs of motherhood and consider whether they want to take on the burden of child rearing in light of their other commitments. However, such women by no means speak for the majority. In the majority of cases, motherhood was an accepted, virtually inevitable, and usually desirable event in the normal progression of a woman's life.

Family Timing: The Typical Pattern

All but a handful of women counted on getting married within a few years of finishing their educations, whether this meant high school or college, and then having children within the first two or three years of marriage. As they explained, this was just what was expected.

Nancy Shine, a high-school graduate, was married at twenty, and became a mother at twenty-two.

> That's the way things were in those days. If you didn't have a baby within a year of getting married then you were sterile or something was wrong with you. Really, there was a lot of pressure, even though it was unspoken. If you didn't get married three years after high school everyone would think, "My God, what's the matter with her?" You were an old maid by twenty-one. Really, thank God that's changed.

Lisa Carr, college-educated, married at twenty-three and became a mother at twenty-six.

> I don't think at that particular point, when we first got married, my husband and I thought about when to have kids. So what we did, in essence, was copy exactly what our friends were doing. They were all married. They had all gotten married and then taught for two years and then got pregnant. So I knew

three years was the maximum I was going to teach and then get pregnant. I don't think we even discussed it. It was just something we knew would happen because it was just a pattern.

As one other mother summed up "There was very much a clear order to these things."

The majority of women followed this order with little deviation: for them, there were few surprises. The average age at which the women were married was twenty-three; as expected, those with only high-school educations married somewhat earlier (average age, 21). The average age of mothers at the birth of their first child was 25.8 years. Again, as expected, high school graduates gave birth several years earlier than those with college educations. The underlying pattern, though, was the same: finish your education; wait a year or two; marry; and then wait a couple of years before starting a family. Only ten women (14 percent) waited until thirty to have their first child. As a group, these ten women married later than the majority (average age, twenty-six), were more highly educated (seven of the ten had college degrees as opposed to only 40 percent of the whole sample), and held more high-status jobs (80 percent were professionals or technical workers compared to 44 percent of all respondents). Even the majority of college-educated women and professionals, however, married and had children more or less according to the standard pattern. Only 24 percent (*n*=18) waited four or more years after they were married to become parents. Seventy percent were mothers within the first three years of their marriages.

Deviations from the Norm

It is interesting to take a more careful look at the women whose lives have departed from these seemingly standard notions of a correct, if predetermined, order. First, at least six women became pregnant earlier than expected, while they were still single.[8] All these women subsequently married the fathers of their babies and for a while tried to live up to the ideal that children should be raised by two parents. Marriages under such pressures being notoriously bad risks, five of the six were divorced or separated from their spouses within ten years. By itself, this small group accounts for over 70 percent of all the respondents who have been married more than once. In addition to this group, a larger number of women, the "delayed child bearers," became mothers later than they had expected. Interestingly, it was one cohort, women who were war babies (that is, born between 1941 and 1945) that tended to delay both marriage and child bearing. For whatever reasons (the pursuit of a career, the lack of an available partner, the decision to wait until a husband's education or job training was completed, setting the goal of purchasing a house before starting a family, and so forth) well over two-thirds (71 percent) of the twenty-five women in this age cohort became parents after the age of twenty-five in contrast to approximately half of the women who were either younger or older—even though women of all ages had shared similar expectations about the timing of family events.[9] Finally, another 10 percent of the women delayed child bearing not out of any choice, but because of fertility problems. On the average, these women were married more than seven years before finally carrying a baby to term.

The women who became mothers either earlier or later than the average shared the feeling that their lives have unfolded in an unusual manner. They viewed themselves as being different from their peers. While some had a work colleague or friend who had a baby at the same time they did, for the most part, they felt other women followed a more standard course. However, in at least some respects, these women appear neither to harbor regrets nor to have gained greater satisfaction from their family timing than those whose lives have supposedly been more on schedule. This is primarily because so many women, regardless of how old they were when they married and had their first child, seemed ambivalent about whether there is ever a perfect time to become a parent. Life is not perfect, they acknowledged; of course, there are always tradeoffs and compromises. Although they could now see the pluses and minuses for doing things the way they did, they could also see the advantages and disadvantages of most any family-timing pattern.

Hindsight: The Tradeoffs between Early and Late Childbearing

Looking back on their timing, a number of women claim they would arrange things differently if they had the opportunity to start over again today. Over 60 percent of those who had children before the age of twenty-five and almost a third of the women who had children early in marriage (within less than three years) said they would now have postponed child-bearing until later in their lives. Their reservations about timing were most apparent in the ways they would counsel their own children to take more time, to establish careers, travel, "find themselves," and learn to relate to their spouses not only as two parents but as two relatively unburdened adults. The notion of saving time for oneself, with its assumption that women can and maybe even should do other things before becoming responsible for another being, was attributed to the women's movement and perceived as a major and welcome shift in the societal and religious pressures placed on young adults. While there were some women, particularly well-educated mothers now in their early to mid-thirties, who felt they had benefited from this notion, the majority of women presented it as an option which came into being too late for them. One Catholic woman, for example, who followed the dictates of her church and become a mother within the first year of her marriage, would advise others to time things quite differently. She explained her reasons:

> I think that women should have more time to experience the fulfillment of a career so that when they do have children their minds may not be so restless....I don't want this to sound like I resent having my children or that they took my career away from me; I don't want it to sound that way because that's not how I really feel. But ideally, I think that if a new parent is a little bit older and has had a chance not to be so restless or unsettled it's better. When I first got married, my life was a whirlwind. I met Frank when I was twenty and at twenty-two we were engaged and at twenty-three we were married and at twenty-four we were new parents and at twenty-five we had our second child and at twenty-six we had our third....I didn't have the chance to breathe...to get my body and soul together and be on the right track. My body was racing; my soul wanted the quiet.

In addition to time to establish a career and personal goals as a young adult, women recognized the advantages for a marriage of waiting to have a child. As one mother said:

> The benfits of having a child later is that your marriage has already gone past the crucial point. Your marriage is pretty secure. You've done a lot of things together and I think at that point in your life there is a need for something more than each other. You need something else, a goal to strive for, another person, something. That's why we decided we wanted a child.

In spite of the acknowledged advantages of waiting, however, several women suggested that having a lot of unencumbered time both before marriage and then as a married childless couple might also make it more difficult to make the transition to parenthood. Waiting, you have more time to taste the freedoms you must give up to raise a child. While respondents who waited until their late twenties and early thirties to give birth were by and large content with their decisions, they perhaps most strongly felt the differences between being childless and not. As Jan Lesser, who was married ten years before having a daughter, related:

> When you're older, you've already had a taste of the world and trips and things and you kind of miss all the extra things in a way. You love your child and everything, but there is a part that's almost gone, it's ended.

An underlying theme running through women's discussions of the trade-offs involved in different family-timing patterns was their common perception that, no matter when you first become a mother, it is difficult to incorporate a child into your life. Even under the best of circumstances, the demands of child rearing interfere with and alter what you have been able to accomplish and enjoy as a nonparent. Yet women took care to explain that recognizing such changes and even some losses was not the same as regretting having a child. They acknowledged tradeoffs without feeling they had been cheated or followed the wrong path.

The Dangers of Waiting Too Long

Although most advocated waiting some time before starting a family, many mothers were concerned about what they viewed as a popular trend toward having children late in life. Even though they dismissed early childbearing as an old fashioned and no longer desirable pattern, they were leary about women waiting until thirty or later to give birth. One respondent surmised, "It would be too easy to become selfish and set in your ways." As a result, there was a fairly circumscribed number of years which most women presented as the "right" time to become a mother. While it was deemed acceptable, if not better, to wait until your mid- to late twenties to gain some time for yourself, delaying beyond that point was viewed as dangerous. The perceived dangers were both physical and psychological in nature. First, women were concerned about medical reports of increased chances of fertility problems with advancing maternal age (even though the seriousness of such problems has been disputed).[10] Second, they perceived that adults experience declines in energy levels and emotional flexibility in their thirties and beyond. "I could never cope with little ones now," more than one woman in her thirties remarked. Given these considerations, most women thought it best to have a child before thirty, including several mothers who had waited until later themselves.

In a book titled *Sooner or Later,* psychologists Pamela Daniels and Kathy Weingarten point out that family-timing decisions have ramifications that are not confined to the time when men and women are in the active stages of child rearing, but apparent later in life as well.[11] Having children late means you gain time alone before becoming a parent, but this gain may necessitate a loss at the other end of the life cycle—when you are forty-five and still dealing with the problems of school-age children or if you are called upon to cope with the demands of young children and the care of aging parents at the same time. The women here were generally too young to have personally experienced such tradeoffs; they neither anticipated nor weighed the consequences of family timing on such a long-term basis.

One ramification of later childbearing was already apparent, though, and that was the tendency of women who became mothers at thirty or beyond to have fewer children than they had expected and fewer than their counterparts who gave birth at an earlier point in their lives. The ten women who became mothers over thirty were unusual not only in when they had their first child, but in how they thought about subsequent children as well. These ten women account for 62 percent, or eight out the thirteen women, who had only one child. Jan Lesser's experience was typical of that of the delayed childbearers as a group. In putting off having her first child, she also wound up limiting the size of her family. Although she originally planned on having two children, at thirty-six, she feels she will now have to limit her family to only one child. As she recounted:

> I can't really say how we decided to make it one. At this point, I feel I'm really too old to have another. Besides, with one, I was able to get back working and I like my work. I like working two or three days a week and with my work situation it would be impossible with two children.

While Mrs. Lesser appeared to be quite satisfied with her situation, her experience also bears out some of the prejudices about late childbearing held by a larger number of respondents. First, there are still strong norms against having an only child. Limiting one's family to one child was portrayed as something done out of constraint, because of fertility or marital problems, or out of a somewhat misguided and "selfish" career orientation. Without being directly asked, more than 15 percent of the women brought up the case of the "poor," "maladjusted" only child of some dual-career couple they knew. In spite of a growing body of research documenting the high achievement levels and relative emotional stability of only children, and particularly those from middle-income backgrounds,[12] even mothers with one child tended to describe their son or daughter in counterpoint to our worst stereotypes—"Our child is a very well-adjusted, happy child, for an only child."

Perhaps more importantly, however, Mrs. Lesser balanced the decision of whether to have more than one child, at least in part, against her commitment to employment. This approach worried less career-oriented women. They feared that women not only become set in their ways if they wait until thirty to have a baby, but that they often then find it difficult to maintain the boundary between what was perceived as a legitimate search for personal and career fulfillment, on the one hand, and selfishness on the other. Clearly, this preconception and prejudice has as much, if not more, to do with women's attitudes about maternal employment than it does with family timing issues per se, and it is but one example of the tension which arises when women view the choices and lifestyles of others who have priorities different than their own. While most respondents gave at least lip service to the importance of personal fulfillment and the ideal of women as individuals in their own right, they also expressed concern that some women have placed too great an emphasis on individuality and self-fulfillment, an emphasis which they viewed as antithetical to the highly regarded value of giving to one's family. If such women were prejudiced against only children, they were even more prejudiced against those career-oriented women whom they saw basing decisions to have one child on their work. What choices respondents made for themselves as well as how they view what they perceive as the sometimes selfish choices of others is a topic which will recur throughout the book.

Family Size: Expectations Meet Reality

As noted, irrespective of the age at which they first became mothers, most women had fewer children than they had originally planned for or fantasized about. Typically, lowering expectations to meet reality meant having two children instead of three, three instead of four, and so on. It specifically did not mean having one child. The feeling was, if you were committed to one child, you would automatically have at least one more. Accordingly, half of the women planned on having the fairly standard and socially acceptable number of two or three children. About a quarter of the women wanted between four and seven and approximately an additional 10 percent (most all of whom were from Claremont) thought big, in terms of eight or more: "I walked down the aisle and said to my husband, 'eight children, please.' And he said,'Let's start with one.'" Only 22 percent, however, wound up having more than three children.

It was the rare case in which a woman cut back on family size in order to continue or advance her career; only three or four women even mentioned thinking about employment in this context. In fact, several other reasons were offered for why women had fewer children than expected. In a handful of cases, fertility problems influenced family size. More often, however, women felt that they could not afford the energy, time, or money to sustain as many children as had populated their fantasies. Besides, as several pointed out, while families with four to six children did not seem especially unusual or large while they were growing up, now any mother with more than three children is repeatedly asked, "How do you ever manage to cope with them all?" Financial pressure was the major reason women gave for limiting family size, to the extent that several of the older women suggested that if they had been faced with the economic conditions of the 1980s when they became mothers, they would never have had any children at all. Although it is unlikely that they would really now opt for childlessness, assessments of the economy and a family's personal financial holdings were important factors in determining when many had decided to get pregnant. Couples, particularly those who were married when housing costs and mortgage rates were more within the reach of middle-income families, often waited to start a family until they could afford to buy a home. Before having a child, both working- and middle-class wives would typically work for the specific purpose of being able to save enough for a down payment on a house. As one woman, in her late thirties, related:

We wanted an opportunity, first of all, to buy a house. We had both grown up in two-family homes and we swore we would never have a family when we would have to worry about the downstairs neighbors.... But we couldn't do it today. If it were today, I wouldn't start a family, I wouldn't. I think the times are terrible. Inflation is terrible. It's very hard to buy a house; it's very hard just to get by.

Others echoed similar concerns: "I don't see how people starting out today manage. I don't think I'd ever have a family if I had to do it now." Whether these women would really do things differently if given the opportunity today is really beside the point. Rather, what their response reminds us of is that while many options for women may have expanded over the past several decades, other possibilities are more constrained. The majority of women over thirty-seven owned their own home before their first child was three or four; younger women have typically had to wait longer and some worry whether they will ever be able to afford a house, especially if they are unwilling to combine full-time employment with child rearing.

Family Spacing: The Timing of Subsequent Children

One further issue to address in a discussion of family timing is how parents planned the spacing of subsequent children. However, unlike their shared expectations about becoming mothers and their similar notions about the appropriate timing of first children, no one pattern emerges from women's explanations of family spacing. Family spacing appears to be far more idiosyncratic and based on personal experiences and circumstances.

Unlike the decision about when to start a family, economics did not appear to play a major role in spacing decisions, probably because virtually all the women had husbands who were stably employed at the time they had their first child and whose earnings were rising the longer couples were married. As is widely known, cultural values had an influence on family-spacing patterns. Jews and Protestants were more likely to leave more than two years between children (and to have fewer children) than Catholics. Catholic women were likely to talk about the advantages of having children closer together so that siblings would be close and able to play with each other. In contrast, Jews were more likely to place an emphasis on having time between each child, so that individual children would "get what they deserve" from their parents. A handful of college-educated women mentioned that they had tried to follow popular psychology books such as Burton White's *The First Three Years*, which advises parents to leave at least three years between siblings.[13] In large part, though, second and subsequent children appeared to follow no generally agreed upon time schedule. Some of this unpredictability was due to the fact that more than 15 percent of the women had trouble conceiving (meaning a delay of a year or more) later children, a larger number than had experienced difficulty timing the arrival of their first-borns. But all in all, there was little accord on what spacing was best because women thought there were many tradeoffs involved, both for children and their mothers. (Tradeoffs for fathers usually did not enter into this consideration since the day-to-day tasks of child care were primarily performed by women and thus envisioned as constraints on mothers', not fathers', lives.) For example, one twenty-nine-year-old Catholic mother had three children under six and was pregnant with her fourth, and what she expected was her last, child. She mentioned that she would actually have preferred her children to be spaced even closer, so that they could play more easily together and so that she would already be finished with diapers and infant care by this point in her life. Other mothers told different stories. Some with children spaced as much as three to five years apart said they had wanted more space between births but had become pregnant unexpectedly; others said they wanted less space but had trouble conceiving.

In the midst of these different patterns and assessments of family spacing, one common theme did emerge: the spacing of children was considered not only in terms of possible benefits or problems for children, as developmental psychologists such as Burton White weigh most heavily in their calculations, but also in terms of how child rearing fits into a woman's life. Spacing children closer together means that a mother may have to deal with an infant and toddler in diapers at the same time, but then she will be freed from the period of heaviest child-care responsibilities. Similarly, allowing more space eases the burden on a mother at any one time, but prolongs the number of years of active child rearing. For women who wanted to devote many years to child rearing and who enjoyed being full-time mothers, this was seen as a plus; for women who looked on the preschool years more as a time out or as an interruption from other commitments, it was a drawback. Unlike decisions of whether to have more than one child, plans regarding family spacing were viewed as legitimately based on how a woman framed her employment plans and career aspirations and, in particular, how long she planned on remaining at home providing child care.

Almost parenthetically, it was interesting to note that the increasing availability of contraception was not seen as a major source of change which has occurred over the course of respondents' lives. The luxury of being able to postpone childbearing and reliably plan one's family size is, of course, a relatively modern choice made possible by the effectiveness and acceptability of birth-control measures. However, only a small group of Catholic women in their forties (who were thus already in their twenties during the "sexual revolution" of the sixties) mentioned birth control as a major difference between their generation and the current one. Most of the women—Protestant, Catholic, and Jew alike—had practiced contraception in their marriages, controlling the number and spacing of their offspring. (Indeed, the two women who were most rancorous about their family timing had been advised by doctors that they shouldn't worry about birth control when they first got married since medical problems had made them relatively infertile and they wouldn't conceive for many years. After becoming pregnant right away, one of these women recalled, "I was so angry [with that doctor] I could have put poison in his coffee.") In keeping with the strong expectation most had of mothering, not one woman mentioned that the decision to come off birth control and to start trying to get pregnant was emotionally difficult or stressful.

A few of the delayed childbearers mentioned that they had considered having children at an earlier point in their lives, but had rejected getting pregnant since they had not felt "really ready." Several of these women claimed that they had never really made a decision to get pregnant. Instead, they "sort of became pregnant by accident" or they were "just about ready to decide" to have a child when they found out they were expecting. Several others expressed that they just somehow knew when it was "the right time"; they found it difficult to find the right words to express how this came about, but stated their bodies "sent them a message that it was right," they just got a real "urge" to become a mother. They made it sound less like a conscious choice than some kind of subconscious, almost mystical message from their bodies. Considering that these delayed childbearers were among the most educated and articulate respondents, their difficulty in finding the right words to explain their decision was even more striking. It's almost as if having planned their careers and devoted many years to self-reflection about their lifestyle and marriages, they wanted to inject some romance into their pregnancy decisions. They wanted to avoid having the timing of their child's birth sound like some calculated plan. A few said they would not counsel their own children when to start a family in terms of chronological age or even in terms of their other life commitments, but would encourage them "to listen" to their bodies, to have children "whenever they got the feeling it was the right time."

Final Considerations

If, to this point, it sounds like decisions about when to have a child and how many children to have are unilateral and dependent solely on wives, this is, first, because the primary concern here is with how women think about their lives and, second, because so few women reported that they had any trouble, as a couple, deciding issues regarding family timing and size. There were some discrepancies, to be sure; one husband, for example, wanted to have four children, just like the family he had come from, and his wife wanted two, just like her family of origin. For the most part, these discrepancies seemed to be settled amicably, without major marital difficulties. The couple in this case compromised and had three children. In two other situations, where childbearing was postponed until both members of the couple were in their late thirties, husbands were reportedly a little less eager to become parents and more ambivalent about the expected child than their spouses. In these cases and in general, however, it seemed that once a woman decided the time was right to start a family, there was little dissuading her from becoming pregnant, and no woman reported her husband fighting such a decision.

In closing, one of the most striking features of the women's reflections about their childbearing patterns is the extent to which they adhered to the notion that career demands and constraints on personal lifestyles are insufficient justifications for not having children, or for only having one child. Using that charged word which surfaced time and time again, women referred to these concerns as "selfish." In a provocative article titled "To Breed or Not to Breed," Harry Stein argues that in placing personal considerations above the responsibility to procreate and take on the demanding responsibility for raising children, men and women in their late twenties and thirties have "become the most profoundly selfish generation of adults."[14] His sentiment reflects a fear that too many of this pivotal generation have put "selfish" considerations before their desire or social responsibility to rear children. Yet this fear seems somewhat exaggerated. Those who have chosen such a "selfish" course are more of a minority than we often imagine. They may be, to be sure, a distinct and significant subgroup, composed of the so-called "up-scale"crowd, drawn from the ranks of highly educated and affluent professionals. It is a matter of some concern if such talented individuals, who have reaped the benefits of so many of society's resources and who have so much to offer children, either choose not to become parents or, if they enter into parenthood, think of it as a sacrifice, however noble. But there are two reasons our concerns about a selfish generation and the demise of the commitment to child rearing appear unfounded. First, individuals who opt for childlessness are still only a small minority; motherhood may not be the cultural imperative it once was, but it remains a primary commitment and major life role of the majority of the nation's women. Second, as will soon be illustrated in more detail, most women do not consider being a mother as a self-sacrificing occupation, nor do they view their employment and lives outside the family sphere with such unbridled passion and lack of concern for their more traditional roles as wives and mothers that they can in any way be categorized as "selfish." If the mainstream women here speak for some of the many others like them, we can feel assured that women are continuing to place a value on investing in the next generation. The question which does arise, however, and to which we now turn more directly, is how much are we also investing in mothers' lives, in women's potential to be both child rearers and more.

Notes

1. Interestingly, women interviewed as part of a parallel study of the daughters of elderly parents (also under a grant from the National Science Foundation with Laura Lein as principal investigator) were far more reticent to talk about their lives and far less reflective. As Ann Stueve, who was in charge of this component of the research, reports, not only did more women refuse to participate in this aspect of the research project but the interviews, on the whole, took much less time and yielded material that was less circumspect and rich in nature.

2. Karl Mannheim, *Ideology and Utopia*, New York: Harcourt, Brace & World, 1936, 47.

3. Mannheim, *Ideology and Utopia*.

4. See Mirra Komarovsky, "Female Freshmen View Their Future: Career Salience and Its Correlates," *Sex Roles* 8, *No. 3*, 1982.

5. See Mary Jo Bane, *Here to Stay* and Lois W. Hoffman, "Social Change and Its Effects on Parents and Children: Limitations to Knowledge," *Women: A Developmental Perspective*, Phyllis W. Berman and Estelle Ramsey, Eds., U.S. Department of Health and Human Services, NIH Publication No. 82-2295, April 1982.

6. For an informal, but informative account of sex-role development, see Lotte Pogrebin, *Growing Up Free*, New York: McGraw Hill, 1980.

7. Pogrebin, *Growing Up Free.*

8. It is possible that more women became pregnant out of wedlock but that they were uncomfortable relating this information to an interviewer. Several of the women who recounted such an experience did so only after the initial phase of the interview was over and they were more comfortable and trusting of the interviewer and the interview situation.

9. This cohort difference in when woman gave birth to their first child was significant at the .05 level (Chi-square test).

10. Pamela Daniels and Kathy Weingarten, *Sooner or Later: The Timing of Parenthood in Adult Lives*, New York: W.W. Norton, 1981.

11. Daniels and Weingarten, *Sooner or Later.*

12. See L. Belmont and I.A. Mirolla, "Birth Order, Family Size, and Intelligence," *Science* 182, 1973, 1096-1101; and L.C. Steelman and J.A. Mercy, "Unconfounding the Confluences Model: A Test of Sibship Size and Birth-Order Effects on Intelligence," *American Sociological Review* 45, 1980, 571-582.

13. Burton White, *The First Three Years.*

14. Harry Stein, "To Breed or Not to Breed," *Esquire,* June 1983, 442-445.

4
Expectations of Employment

Just as they planned on following a straight and narrow path to marriage and motherhood, the women interviewed anticipated a simple journey through the world of employment. Most had foreseen paid work as playing only a limited role in their lives; using the same words they applied to their youthful expectations of motherhood, they labeled their expectations of employment as "old fashioned" and "out of the dark ages." Only three women recalled that they had planned on continuing paid jobs while they were raising a family, and they were among the youngest women in the study. Far more often, women took pains to distance themselves from those coming of age in the 1980s, whom they perceive as thinking quite differently than themselves about how employment and child rearing can fit into a woman's life.

Indeed, there is evidence from survey studies to support this perception of social change. Not only are many more women, and mothers in particular, in the labor force than ever before, but teenagers do appear to be planning differently for their futures. In a survey of college freshmen conducted in 1979, for example, almost half of the women questioned by Mirra Komarovsky reported that they expect "to combine family life with a career with a minimum of interruption for childbearing."[1] When she conducted a similar study almost twenty-five years ago, only 12 percent of those surveyed planned on following such a course: most expected that motherhood would naturally supplant employment. This suggests a considerable shift in women's normative expectations about their lives. Overall, the women under study here place themselves, both in chronological age and in values, closer to the teenagers questioned by Komarovsky a generation ago: by and large, they started out with no plans to find ways to integrate paid work into their domestic roles.

Not all the women, however, have experienced the same degree of dissonance between what they grew up believing and what they see before them now. Because of their different personal circumstances, respondents have adapted differently to the changing norms which dictate the types of work today's mothers perform. In the following, I recount how women recall their childhood plans for employment and careers and the extent to which they feel they have changed and accommodated to modern day realities and ideologies regarding women's place in the labor force.

Two Scenarios

In recounting their youthful dreams and expectations, over 80 percent of the women spontaneously related one of two strikingly similar scenarios. Taken together, these two scenarios illustrate the strength of social norms regarding women's roles, and the extent to which women perceive that society and views of women's work have evolved in their lifetimes.

The first scenario, which can be described as *Motherhood Supplants Employment,* detailed a pattern we think of as traditional (although by traditional we typically, and perhaps romantically, mean how we envision life in the post-World War II decades and not what types of labor women historically have had to perform in order to survive). According to this scenario, a woman was expected to marry, have children, and from then on devote her full-time efforts to family and home. As thirty-four-year-old Deborah Sammet responded in answer to a question about how long she thought she would be at home caring for children:

> See, I was of a different generation. I was taught that you work until you got married and then you had children and didn't work any more. You had to stay home and take care of your children and be a good mommy. And, you know, only mothers that were, well, not bad mothers, but who didn't want to be mothers, wanted to be working. All the other mothers who loved their children were home taking care of them. So I really didn't expect to go back to work. I was going to be a mother and take care of my children. And I would stick around the house and clean.

Forty-three percent, or thirty-one women, detailed essentially this same scenario. After the birth of their first child, they imagined that they would retire from the workplace and remain at home, economically dependent upon their presumably successful husbands, now sardonically referred to by them as "Mr. Wonderful" and "the man on the white horse." Two-thirds of those who expected to follow this pattern were thirty-seven years of age or older (the median age of women in the sample). Where only about a quarter of the women under thirty-seven planned on being home "forever," one-half of the older women had no plans for taking a paid job after giving birth.

In the second scenario, which can be described as *Employment as a Contingency,* a greater emphasis was placed on women's paid work, but here, too, employment was portrayed not as a primary life role or commitment, but as a fall back, as a precaution against unforeseeable emergencies or a kind of personal amusement. As above, women who related this scenario expected to quit their jobs to devote full-time to mothering, but in the back of their minds they were aware that one day they might return to paid work, either because they would become bored at home or because (not altogether unrealistically) they foresaw a day when perhaps their husbands would be unable to generate enough income on their own. In viewing women's changing employment patterns, it's easy to neglect how many women growing up in the fifties and sixties planned on having jobs or careers to fall back on. As forty-year-old Janet Kelley, who had always planned on being a teacher, explained:

> I wanted financial security for myself and I know that goes back to the insecurity my parents experienced not having an education. . . . I wanted a family too and I thought in terms of, well, if anything happens to Mr. Wonderful, either he's killed or he dies—I never thought of divorce or anything like that—but if anything happened or I needed a second income or anything, teaching would be the perfect job to fit in with a family. . . . A teaching job was just ideal if you were going to follow the pattern set for you by society that you would grow up and get married. You would first teach and then you would get married and then you would have children and then you wouldn't work. Then you might someday need to go back to work or want to go back. I was sort of the generation that it was okay to go back eventually and so I did. I thought my life was all set. I had the whole thing planned when I was seventeen.

This type of scenario was recounted by thirty-seven women, a number about equal to that of those who spoke in terms of the first scenario. However, this latter group of women was considerably younger. Almost 60 percent of them were under the median age of thirty-seven.[2] In addition to teaching, women presented nursing as the other occupation which was compatible with the demands of child rearing and noted for the ease of reentry after years of full-time mothering. Showing the overwhelming acceptability of these occupations, over half of the women who planned on any career at all thought they would be either teachers or nurses.

Women who spoke in terms of the *Employment as a Contingency* scenario can be divided into two categories. The first is composed of the relatively well-educated daughters of middle-class parents. They counted on going to college or vocational school to learn a profession or trade which they would then practice until they became mothers. When their children were school-age or older, they would again consider a paid job. They were raised thinking that employment could offer some degree of personal gratification and fulfillment, even if it was just assumed it would take a back seat to motherhood and probably serve only as a way to pass some free time when the demands of family ebbed. While half of the women who had only high-school educations expected to be home forever, only about a quarter of the college graduates had similar plans; the majority of these better-educated women thought they would go back to work at some point in their lives. In contrast, the second category of women who related this scenario were from less affluent, more working-class families. They were women, like Janet Kelley, who had experienced economic hardships in their childhood. Some had witnessed their own mothers struggling to combine a breadwinner role with single parenting. As a result, they placed a high value on financial self-sufficiency and since youth had looked upon their own earning potential as an important factor for future financial security.

Despite the differences between the two scenarios, women who spoke in terms of motherhood supplanting employment and those who spoke of employment as a contingency both felt they were describing old fashioned and traditional patterns. Despite the emphasis on employment in the second scenario, the priority was still placed on a mother's work at home. Under the best of circumstances, if marriages remained intact and husbands stayed healthy and successful, the women did not look forward to combining employment with child rearing. Hand in hand with those who described the first scenario, these women, at least for a major portion of their lives, expected to be wives and mothers, first, foremost, and almost exclusively.

Role Models: The Influence of Their Mothers' Work Styles

To what extent were women's expectations regarding employment shaped by what their own mothers did? There is no one clear-cut answer. For example, the two scenarios outlined above, both downplaying the possibility as well as the importance of employment, were reported regardless of whether a woman's own mother was employed. As Claire DuBois remembered:

> I didn't think anything more than I'd have my children and stay home. That's what you did then; it wasn't expected that you would work. Although that's not what I grew up with, because my mother was a career person. She was a trust officer in a bank in my home town and she went back to work when I was in the sixth grade and did very well.

Despite their presenting employment as a "new" option for women, 60 percent of the respondents' mothers had returned to work after having a child; almost 20 percent had done so while children were still preschoolers and almost an additional 25 percent were employed while they were caring for school-age children. Most often, however, as previously mentioned, respondents viewed their mothers' employment as aberrant. In their minds, at least, they were the only kids on the block who didn't have a full-time mother.

This impression may, at least in part, be accurate. Even though many of the older generation worked outside the home at some point in their lives, their forays into the world of employment have generally not been lasting or long-term. Often, they moved in and out of the labor force, as necessitated by the vagaries of family economics. As a result, although many mothers of this prior generation may indeed have work histories, the number of employed women in any given neighborhood or community may not have been large enough to make a visible difference to their daughters; the number who may have placed an emphasis on their paid work appears to have made an even smaller psychic impression.[3] In keeping with our Ozzie-and-Harriet-like portrayals of a full-time homemaker in every house, mothers' employment did seem atypical.

Most often, daughters remembered their employed mothers as victims of their circumstances. Their husbands were dead, unsuccessful in their jobs, drinkers, or in some other way unreliable—or else the family business required that everyone join in the work. It's not so much that mothers had portrayed to their daughters that employment was onerous and unenjoyable; it was more that mothers and daughters just never seemed to talk about it much at all, except in terms of meeting financial needs. Respondents whose mothers had to work expressed pride that their mothers had been able to juggle employment and child rearing. Just one woman viewed her mother as working out of choice. Simply, daughters saw their mothers working because they had to. In some families, grandmothers or other relatives, such as elderly aunts, were on hand to greet children after school and attend to their needs. The women who grew up in such extended family circumstances typically felt that their own mother's employment thus had little impact on their lives. "There was always someone there when I got home," reported one women, "and that was really all that mattered." (When it came time to have their own children, however, few respondents felt they had family who could be called on to help so readily and most—including a few who were raised under such conditions—rejected the idea that other relatives could take a mother's place; more on this later.) In other families, mothers worked around children's schedules and made efforts to be at home whenever youngsters were not in school; these daughters, too, saw mothers' paid work as having little impact on their lives. However, there was a handful of cases in which women did experience maternal employment as a loss. These women had vowed not to work when their own kids were young.

In general, there seems to be no simple way to predict whether maternal employment positively or negatively influenced respondents' feelings about paid work. Some disliked the fact of their mothers' employment, some didn't care much one way or another, and still a few others thought of it in primarily positive terms. The same could be said of having a mother who was a full-time homemaker. While most women with such a past remarked on how they had liked it, there were others who had sensed their mothers' dissatisfaction or felt they should have been doing something different. There was no apparent correlation between whether a woman planned on working and whether or not her own mother had worked. By and large, having an employed mother did not predispose a woman to expect a career of her own.

Some respondents, despite their exposure to the realities which required that their mothers work, simply hoped that they would be luckier and able to find and keep husbands who would support them adequately. Others, more practically minded, drew from their experiences, and made sure they had job skills they could rely on when and if necessary. Except for the unusual case, though, mothers' jobs were not viewed as careers, and daughters, in viewing their mothers' lives, did not predict that they one day might also be working, much less that they might be employed not only for money but for personal satisfaction as well.

In part, this discounting of a mother's employment can be related to the relatively modern notion that a job should be personally fulfilling. Beyond a few nurses and teachers and a handful of other such skilled workers (nine in all), most of the respondents' mothers were in dead-end, low-paying jobs, jobs to which their daughters by no means aspired. In addition, some worked hard in family stores and businesses but never really brought home a separate paycheck. At times, this work was almost invisible. When one woman was asked if her mother worked, she at first replied no. After thinking about it a little longer, she changed her answer to yes—her mother spent several hours every day working at the family grocery store, but it was her father who supposedly worked in and ran the business.

In sum, mothers' employment appeared to have little effect on daughters' expectations. Despite the fact that almost half of their mothers worked (at least for a time) while they were youngsters, just about all the women planned on being at home, either for a prolonged period while their children were growing up or for the rest of their lives. These were not women who entertained grandiose notions of their future jobs or careers.

Placing Themselves in Context: Followers, Straddlers, and Departers

Later in this work, women's actual employment patterns and current arrangements are detailed along with the extent to which their youthful expectations have been borne out. What is most interest here is that in talking about the changing norms surrounding women's employment and child-rearing roles, the women situated themselves historically somewhere between the values and norms they associate with their youth and what they perceive as modern ideologies, with their emphasis on the importance of paid work. Although heretofore the women collectively have been referred to as a pivotal generation, upon closer examination some diversity becomes apparent. It is possible to distinguish three subgroups. Each subgroup differs with respect to where women position themselves historically—what time they identify as their own—and to how much they feel they have been able to accommodate to social changes over the last two decades. Which subgroup a woman identifies with is dependent upon two main factors: her chronological age, which marks when social changes have occurred in her life and structures how open she is to incorporating new ways of conceptualizing her roles, and her level of education, which not only influences her values and priorities but also shapes what opportunities and possibilities have been available to her.

The first group of women can be thought of as "followers." These twenty-two women not only talked about what it was like to grow up prior to the days of women's liberation, but their present notions of being a woman and mother continue to closely parallel the dreams and expectations of their youth. Followers tend to identify with what they term the "past generation." In the midst of change, they see themselves still adhering to many of the values and conceptions of women's roles they held when they were young. As forty-three-year-old Susan Klein explained in response to a question about whether she ever imagined herself getting a paid job:

> No. I don't think I'll ever work. Because I was brought up in the old school where you married and that was it. You didn't expect to work. I can remember when I was a kid if a girl got married it automatically meant her job was terminated.... Now that never happens. Girls don't even quit now when they have babies. They take a leave of absence. The whole society is different now. So that I think I'm still, well, I'm still old enough to be a part of that.

While some followers have returned to work, or plan to when their children are older, they see themselves as following an expected and traditional pattern. Either they planned to be full-time mothers or they thought of a paid job only as something to "fall back on." Half of the women who are followers explained their youthful expectations in terms of the first scenario, *Motherhood Supplants Employment,* and the other half thought in terms of *Employment as a Contingency.* As a group, followers do not perceive themselves as having departed from their original notions about the importance and priority of mothering in a woman's life.

Almost twice as many followers were over the median age of thirty-seven as were younger (64 percent as opposed to 36 percent). The average age of followers was thirty-nine. In addition, over one half (54 percent) of the women with only high-school educations thought of themselves as followers in contrast to only 7 percent of those who had obtained college degrees. Finally, because the residents of Green Haven were more highly educated than those who live in Claremont, a greater proportion of followers make their home in the more working-class town of Claremont (almost two-thirds of the followers reside there).

Unlike the followers, about an additional one-third of the respondents viewed themselves as "departers," as part of a generation which has broken away from the patterns and norms of the past. As a group, departers see themselves as leading lives significantly different from those of their mothers and also different from their own youthful images and stereotypes of what adulthood would entail. While they might at one time have shared expectations similar to those held by the followers (indeed, they did share the same scenarios), departers now place themselves within a new time and context. Primarily, this means that departers have come to reassess the importance of women's work outside the home and to place a higher value on women's workplace involvements and career potentials.

A handful of departers seemed always to have set themselves apart from the accepted norm in some way. Even though they might have relied on stereotypic scenarios to illustrate how things were when they were growing up, they described themselves as being different from the crowd; they planned on having some kind of career. Few, however, went to the extent of planning long-range goals or even considering how they would combine employment and child rearing. For most departers, employment only emerged as a major factor in their self-definition after they had been exposed to the workplace as adults. Departers were no more likely than followers to have mothers who worked; if anything, a few more of their mothers were full-time homemakers. However, after working a number of years before getting married, and then more years after marriage, departers found that their careers had become more important to them than they had once expected. Judy Kiley, for instance, now works as a fashion designer. Although she always had some idea of studying for a profession, her job increased in personal value the longer she worked before becoming a mother. As she recalled:

> I never really thought about what I would do. That sounds really strange.... We never really talked about careers when we were growing up, not at all. My father was very much against me going to design school—he really thought it was a waste and I would probably just get married and I wouldn't use my education. There was a really big scene in my house when I decided to go to school. I more or less had to fight to go to school. But I really didn't think that much ahead about how I would be using the education I had. It was something I wanted to do at the time and that was it. But long-term goals, I don't really think I had any at that time....It was only later that my work became important to me.

Deborah Hartmann had a similar experience. As she told it:

> When I was growing up and I was in college, I assumed that I would stop teaching when I had my children and then maybe I would return to teaching. But, by the time it came the moment for me to have my child, my teaching had become sufficiently important to me, and apparently always had been, that I never wanted to leave.

Well over half of the departers found that employment had become so important to them that, when they became mothers, they did not want to retire from the workplace. Like followers, as youngsters, departers were equally likely to have expected to be at home full-time (*Motherhood Supplants Employment*) or to think about employment just as a possible escape or safety valve (*Employment as a Contingency*). Unlike followers, however, over the course of their young adult, preparenting years, they came to think of employment in different terms. In short, they rejected the scenarios of their youth.

On the average, departers were more likely to have college degrees (61 percent) than high-school educations (22 percent, with the remaining 17 percent having some college or technical training). Over 70 percent of the departers were below the median age, as opposed to 36 percent of the followers. Age and education, though, were not the only factors which determined whether a woman thought of herself as a departer. Also important were family timing—whether a woman had a baby early or late, and marital status—whether or not a woman's marriage had ever been in jeopardy. Deborah Hartmann, for example, credited her increased commitment to paid work to the fact that she didn't marry until she was in her late twenties: "I married late—later than most people my age. I'm an older mother, too. So in one sense, I was never trapped by the myths I might have entertained at one point in my life." Whether the delays in marriage and childbearing changed a woman's outlook or whether a changed outlook resulted in a woman putting off these events is unclear; there is not sufficient evidence to attribute such causality. But it was apparent that the two went hand in hand.

A few women who were departers had their babies more "on schedule," if not earlier than others. Most of these women, however, had been through what could be termed a radicalizing experience: either their marriages had broken up and they were forced into the breadwinner role as a single parent or their marriages remained intact but their husbands were unable to support the family, usually for health reasons. In these cases, women presented such an event as being the catalyst for their change of mind. Because of what they had been through and pushed into, the women were forced into rethinking their roles as wives, mothers, and employees. In the process of doing so, they began to think of themselves differently, as both beneficiaries of the women's movement and part of a new generation of women.

Significantly, not all the departers were employed at the time of their interviews. In fact, several women who were not employed spoke of how they were at home (temporarily) because "that's the place I know I should be now, with my children." These women, however, not only had plans to return to jobs at some point in the future but they also retained a sense of how important their jobs were and how much their careers had come to mean to them. Even though they were unemployed, they still thought of themselves as social workers, teachers, secretaries, and the like. The distinguishing feature of departers, and a point we will return to later, is that they are women, employed or not, who share a sense of commitment to employment not as a "fall back" but as an essential part of their lives and their self-definition.

The final group of respondents, the "straddlers," located themselves somewhere between departers and followers. They viewed themselves as caught "in the middle," between the norms and expectations of their youth and the realities and new ideas which they have encountered in their adult lives. (See table 4-1 at the end of the chapter for a comparison of followers, straddlers, and departers by demographic variables.) Thirty-four year-old Judy Laufer provided a good description of the ambivalence and sense of displacement felt by straddlers.

> People in my age group are sort of in the middle. We were through with adolescence by the time the women's movement really became important or significant or visible, and a lot of stuff happens in adolescence and there just wasn't the women's movement there as a support. So I think we bought a lot of the old fashioned stuff. But then we weren't too far gone that we couldn't change as the women's movement came in and sort of verified some of the things that we felt but couldn't articulate. I've always felt a real tension...a sense of not really knowing where I belong because I certainly don't feel I belong with my mother's generation. I never totally bought the thing that way, and yet I don't feel that kind of kinship with a lot of other women who have grown up and gone through their adolescence at a time when a lot of things were valid.

In a number of respects, straddlers' perceptions of themselves as "women in the middle" were accurate. As a group, they were older than "departers" (most often in their mid- to late thirties), but younger than followers. Similarly, while they were better educated than followers, they were somewhat less educated than departers; about half had gone to college and half had not. Straddlers were also fairly even split in terms of where they live. Whereas more followers lived in Claremont and more departers resided in Green Haven, about the same number of straddlers lived in each town (ten in Green Haven, twelve in Claremont). What came through most in the interviews with straddlers was their sense of discomfort and ambivalence—not only don't they know whether they are more like their mothers or like the current younger generation, but they also don't really know which group they would rather be like. In short, both followers and departers had fairly firm convictions about the place of mothering and employment in a woman's life. Straddlers, on the other hand, were less certain of the correct answers. This lack of certainty was evident throughout their interviews. While followers and departers were about equally likely to come out with assertions about what women should do, what children truly need from their parents, women's employment, and women's unpaid family and community work, straddlers were more hesitant to make any claims, either for themselves or for others. As a result, of all the respondents, they were the least likely to be sure of their own decisions, and the least likely to treat the decisions and work-family arrangements of other women with derision or contempt.

Table 4-1
A Pivotal Generation and Its Subgroups: Followers, Straddlers, and Departers by Selected Demographic Characteristics

	Followers	*Straddlers*	*Departers*
Median Age			
Under 37	36% (8)	40% (9)	70% (16)
37+	64% (14)	59% (13)	30% (7)
Education			
High school graduates	60% (13)	27% (6)	22% (5)
Some college/technical	18% (4)	27% (6)	17% (4)
College graduates	23% (5)	45% (10)	61% (14)
Residence			
Claremont	64% (14)	55% (12)	39% (9)
Green Haven	36% (8)	45% (10)	61% (14)
Scenario Presented (of the 54 which were codable)			
"Motherhood–Career Termination"	50% (11)	50% (8)	42% (8)
"Motherhood–Career as a Fall Back"	50% (11)	50% (8)	42% (8)
Average Age	40 years	38 years	35 years

Note: Data on characteristics missing for seven participants.

These three distinctions among women of the pivotal generation help illustrate that social change is a gradual process, where individuals incorporate new ideologies and circumstances into their lives and understandings at different rates, depending on their historical and social positions. Even among so-called mainstream women of this one generation, there are essential differences which shape individual life experiences and which temper the impact of what has often been described as the "employment revolution." Having now considered how the women place themselves historically and how they recall their youthful expectations of the place motherhood and employment would have in their lives, let us proceed to how women think about their current commitments to work and family and how they structure their days.

Notes

1. Mirra Komarovsky, "Female Freshmen View Their Futures."
2. Fifty-nine of the interviews contained enough material to piece together either Scenario I, *Motherhood Supplants Employment,* or Scenario II, *Employment as a Contingency.* Of the remaining fifteen, three women spoke in terms of a more modern scenario; they expected to take only a short time out for childbearing. The rest of the interviews were uncodable, in most cases because when respondents were asked to recall how they

thought about employment and child rearing, they responded, "I never thought about it at all." The following is a cross-tabulation of the two scenarios by age of respondents:

	Scenario I	Scenario II
Under 37 years	34% (11)	59% (16)
37 and over	66% (21)	41% (11)

3. This analysis of why mothers' employment seemed almost invisible was spawned by a conversation with Mary Jo Bane, Summer 1982.

Part III
The Place and Meaning of Motherhood and Employment

5
The Quality-versus-Quantity Debate

Judy Laufer, the mother of a two-year old, remained on her job as a social worker for the first year of her son's life, but recently decided to stay home, at least for a while.

I really believe that taking care of small children, the whole experience of pregnancy, birth, and the caring that goes into it, has given me a real sense of what's important in living. One of the things I try to do when I have some major decision to face (and probably it comes from working with old people as long as I have) is to picture myself on my deathbed. I ask myself, "At this point in my life, do I feel satisfied with the life I've led or do I feel, my God, I should have done this or that?" In making the decision that I would quit my job and stay home with Jason, I knew that he would never be small again and that this particular time when he's a toddler and he wants me around is really a limited period of time, even though when you're in the midst of it, it feels like it could go on forever. But I can't get this time back again, not ever.

Pam McFeeley, whose children range in age from one to nine, was planning to go back to work in a few years, whether or not she can find a job as a teacher.

I think there is no greater challenge in the world than being a mother, I really do. I don't think there is anything more fulfilling, to do it well. I really believe in motherhood. It isn't easy, it's a hard job. It's very rewarding, when you see just little successes. I can't think of a job that demands more. I mean, I've had a lot of different jobs. I've had exposure to different things. And I don't know of any job that would incorporate more talents to be really able to do them all well. Running a household you get the business aspect of it, but I still think of cleaning as least important. I mean, sure I like a clean bathroom and things tidied up, but cleaning is like the back thing for me. To be able to listen to kids—and I'm not saying that I do it all the time, I lose my temper sometimes—but to really listen, I just think it's the greatest challenge there could ever be. All my kids have different personalities, and it's so important to look at each or all four of them and remind yourself they're all different, and you have to treat them differently. Even though you have certain standards, they have different needs. If I go back to teaching, I would be much, much better than I ever was before I had children. I could bring much more to it. I would be a lot tougher in a lot of ways.

Ann Ellman, the mother of two, was five months pregnant at the time she was interviewed. A former school teacher, she spent many hours each day repairing and decorating the old house into which her family recently moved.

> I've been going through this thing lately with a sense of the women's movement giving me a complex about Supermom can do everything. You know, you can go to work, you can do it all....And before I was pregnant, I felt I could do both, even when I had more than one child. I thought I'd be able to go back to school now and start planning a career change and then get into some job full-time....And for a while there I kind of said anybody can take care of kids and my children don't care whether it's me or the woman down the street. It really wouldn't make any difference as long as somebody was amusing them and feeding them. But now I think it does make a difference and I see that. Where there are little things I want to do with them; if they get any bad habits, I want to have given them to them and not have to say, look what they've picked up from here, there, or wherever. You know, I want to be solely responsible for their growth. I want to have control over it in that sense.

This chapter is primarily about the place of mothering in women's lives. It considers what mothers feel it is important to give to their children and what they perceive they get back in return for their investments in child rearing. As the above quotes illustrate, however, women's feelings about employment and child rearing are often so entwined that it is almost impossible to discuss one without also mentioning the other. Typically, women explain their commitments as mothers in counterpoint to their commitments to paid work. Similarly, they relate the rewards and satisfactions as well as the stresses of employment in terms of their impact on the time available for family responsibilities. That a tension exists between the demands of paid work and those of child rearing is seen as virtually inevitable. Despite or even because of this tension, women not only experiment with different ways of balancing paid and unpaid work, but, in the process of doing so, they often have come to a deeper understanding of what is important for themselves and for their families.

In opening a discussion of women in their role as mothers, it is therefore necessary to acknowledge the extent to which paid work comprises a critical portion of the context in which child rearing takes place. First, recall that 58 percent of the mothers interviewed were employed. Furthermore, an even higher figure (65 percent) reported that they would prefer to work even if they were not constrained to do so because of financial pressures. In addition, virtually all the women had been employed before becoming mothers, often for up to ten years before giving birth. Ninety-five percent expected to be employed full-time five to ten years hence. On the one hand, it is possible to interpret these statistics as signifying that women's investments in mothering are on the decline, that women will spend less and less time tending children and that the beckoning workplace will overshadow the obligations and rewards of child rearing. Certainly it is already apparent that women's participation in the labor force has reshaped the contours of the maternal role, shortening the number of years women devote solely to being mothers. As is the case nation-wide, fully two-thirds of the women in this study had returned to work before their youngest child had entered first grade.

Yet to use these figures to argue that employment is supplanting the place of child rearing in women's lives is inaccurate and an oversimplification of the issues. The problem modern mothers face is not to choose between paid work or unpaid family work but rather to find ways of integrating the two, of creating a viable synthesis. By emphasizing employment, the above statistics only tell one part of the story. For example, by continuously highlighting the number of mothers who are employed, we have tended to deemphasize the number of women who continue to be at home for all or part of the day—at least for that portion of their lives they are raising young children.[1] We need to remember that while three-fifths of the mothers were employed, the other two-fifths were not; they were full-time homemakers. Moreover, and perhaps more importantly, even of those mothers who were employed, most were not working full-time. Seventy percent of the employed women held part-time jobs; only twelve women had full-time positions. Although a majority of women would prefer to be employed, only 15 percent would opt for full-time employment (these were the same women, minus one, who were actually working thirty-five or more hours a week). In addition, while a total of forty-three women had worked full- or part-time for at least part of the year during which they were inter-viewed, only twenty-seven women (36 percent) continued to work throughout the summer, after their children's school year had ended, and only seven women worked full-time during the summer vacation months. Thus, it is criti-cal to look at the distinction between "labor force participation"—whether or not a woman has been employed—and what has been termed "labor force attachment," that is, the extent to which a woman's labor force involvement is substantial and permanent. As George Masnick and Mary Jo Bane document, there is some evidence to suggest that women's labor force attachment, like their labor force participation, is on the increase. However, here the change is far from dramatic. Women continue to limit their employment and the primary reason they do is so that they can continue to spend time with their children.[2]

Mothers continue to mold their employment schedules around their family responsibilities. Motherhood continues to alter how a woman feels about her job and her career potential. Ask an employed mother what are some of the benefits of the job she has and she is most likely to respond with reasons such as "The hours are good for my family," "I can take time off in case my family needs me," "It's flexible," "I'm able to buy my kids the few extras they want," and also (the absence makes the heart grow fonder rationale) "It's good to get away from my house and the kids for a while, it make me appreciate my family so much more." Whether to work, how much to work, when to work, and at times, even what kind of work to take are all questions considered in light of how a mother assesses the needs of her children and what she feels she must do to maintain an acceptable quality of family life. Certainly there exist some female executives and professionals who see their jobs in more career-oriented terms, but for women in the mainstream, women with primarily low- to middle-range, nonglamorous jobs, paid work is most often first described in terms of family. To the extent that such women feel they have some choice over whether they have to combine employment with child rearing— that is, whether they think their households can get by without additional income—they base their decisions around what they should be doing for their families.

This does not imply that employment, by being relegated to second place, at least while a woman has young children, has little impact or meaning. Too often, we view the employment choices of women and assume an all-or-nothing situation exists; either a woman is invested in a full-time, demanding, career-ladder job or she has a little investment in the labor force and gets, at best, only a slight sense of satisfaction from her paid work. We mistakenly assume that without a continuous commitment to full-time employment or a high-status career, there is little to be gained from employment and those who do not live up to these standards of the male work-world miss out on most of the rewards and pleasures of the workplace. This is not true, and the next chapter details what women perceive they gain from their involvements in paid work. However, before we can really understand the dynamics or importance of employment for mothers, it is essential to look at how women think about family needs and family time, or, what they think it means to be a good mother today.

Definitions of Good Mothering

Our collective image of what it means to be a good mother has lost much of its vividness and clarity over the past several decades. That it is necessary to ask what middle-American women see as good mothering is, in itself, a reflection of our uncertainty. Do contemporary mothers, some of whom are employed and some of whom are full-time homemakers, agree on the boundaries and requisites of good mothering? To address this question, it is helpful to take a step back in time.

Not too long ago, as the mothers of today were reaching maturity, it seemed relatively easy to answer the question at hand. Indeed, the question itself would have seemed superfluous. We, as a society, shared a certain image of what mothering was all about, at least for the large number of white women in the so-called middle mass. While the rich could buy out of whatever child-rearing chores they viewed as particularly onerous or unpleasant and the poor were excused from living up to more middle-class conventions, for women in the mainstream what went into being a mother was pretty clear. Mothers were expected to be the primary caretakers of their families and homes. Responsible for meeting the physical and psychic needs of their youngsters, they were in charge of such chores as cooking, feeding, cleaning, and supervising children at play. Yet even beyond any list of specific duties, we shared a portrait of mothers being there, always available, whether to encourage and witness a baby's first words and steps, to help a toddler make the transition from diapers to potty chair, to comfort a preschooler with a skinned knee or wounded ego, or to greet an older child walking in the door after school and lend a sympathetic ear. Compared to vacuuming, doing the laundry, and other homemaking duties, these latter aspects of child rearing have been imbued in our minds with deeper shades of emotion. Women were brought up thinking that mothers were supposed to be there, so they could be participants in the spontaneous and special moments which occasionally arise as well as the more routine details of children's lives. Any one separate interaction between mother and child might sound rather humdrum and unessential. (Witness how many have poked fun at mothers' worries and conversations about skinned knees, bowel habits, swimming lessons, and the other assorted snags and realities of raising children.) Taken together, however, such encounters constituted an important part of what we thought went into being a good mother. Furthermore, not only was full-time mothering a long-term occupation, but the years a woman spent child rearing were by and large considered her most productive ones.

This image of mothering was repeatedly confirmed and solidified, most notably in a succession of how-to books for parents. Psychiatrists and psychologists, particularly those with a psychoanalytic bent, drew upon case histories of children separated from their mothers (usually for reasons of war or extensive hospitalization) and warned of the dangers of "maternal deprivation." Even Dr. Spock, who by now has changed his tune considerably, counseled women on the importance of being there and advised mothers to put off other commitments until their children were older.[3] Such assertions were based on the assumption that each separate encounter is crucial for a child's well-being and healthy development, and, furthermore, that it is the cumulative effect of constant daily interactions which cements what has been portrayed as the all-important bond between mothers and their offspring.

So long as the great majority of mothers remained full-time homemakers (and so long as the majority of them remained, at least on the surface, content with their role), there was little reason or impetus to question whether this assumption was accurate. As more mothers entered the labor force and as more women came forward to speak of their discontent with being confined to their homes and child rearing, however, doubts began to surface about whether a good mother should solely be defined as one who is at the beck and call of her family. Indeed, women were warned, perhaps "excessive" maternal attention was at the root of children's problems. In the midst of the social changes of the late sixties and seventies, as women's roles increasingly became a legitimate topic of conversation, our prior image of mothering blurred. We became less certain of what we meant by being a good mother. Even the experts began to disagree.

We were reminded that, rather than being written in stone, the ideal of full-time mothering was a product of a particular time and context. Throughout history, women rarely have had the luxury to give so much time and attention to children; survival necessitated that they work in fields or in factories, or that they spend far more hours just attending to household duties. Unfortunately for those looking for easy answers, however, it proved difficult to extrapolate from history and come up with a simple formula for determining what children truly need from their mothers in contemporary society. Likewise, it was impossible to transfer to our context models of communal child rearing, such as exist on the kibbutz, which have worked elsewhere. Our perceptions of children's needs (and the future we are preparing our children for) are as much a reflection of the society in which we live as are the demands of women's work. Therefore, we were left searching for something which would work for us, not something which seemed right for a different time or in some other place.[4]

The Rise of the Quality–Quantity Debate

Many of the complexities of the links between women's work and child rearing were soon subsumed in a growing public debate. In the midst of this debate, the preferences and values of women in the mainstream were often lost among accounts of the rising number of women professionals, single mothers, and so on. Using black and white distinctions which were calculated to sell copy and gain attention, self-professed experts began to argue whether it was the quantity—the total amount and uninterrupted nature of the time mothers spent with children, or the quality—specific and hopefully productive interactions which could take place within circumscribed time periods—which truly mattered. If, quality-time adherents suggested, a mother was able to set aside some special time each day or each week for her children, did she still need to devote so great a total amount of hours to child rearing as many of us had been brought up to expect? At times, this argument has been carried to its rather illogical extreme. Who could disagree that it is better for children to spend a happy and full hour each day talking and playing with a mother who has worked outside the home all day and is satisfied with her dual commitments than it is for them to spend an entire day with a parent who is miserable, a prisoner in her own home, and who has no interest in sharing good times with her family?

Quality time quickly became a slogan associated with the women's movement. At best, it served a timely and important purpose. It was used to support women who, either out of choice or constraint, found that their paid jobs kept them from living up to their "preliberated" notions of being good mothers. Magazines directed at audiences of working mothers and workshops designed to help women sort through employment-family conflicts latched on to the attractive and time-efficient notion of quality time. Reserving time after dinner to talk alone with each child was presented as a way to make up for not being there after school; planning special family outings on Saturday compensated for lost time during the week. In so far as it was legitimate to encourage women to become financially independent and expand their horizons as well as to support those mothers who were forced to work, it was crucial to revise our image of mothering and develop an ideology which minimized the importance of women being mothers, first and foremost, twenty-four hours a day. At the very least, it was important to support the efforts of employed mothers and reduce their guilt and anxieties about not living up to their earlier expectations of motherhood.

At its worst, however, quality time was a rallying cry used to gloss over some very difficult questions. For a while, when the rhetoric of the women's movement was at its strongest, questioning the advisability or even the limits of what was meant by quality time opened oneself up to charges of being anti-feminist, as did Selma Fraiberg when she published her book, *Every Child's Birthright: In Defense of Mothering.*[5] Over the years, it has proven difficult to demonstrate whether quality time is reasonable or whether it really works. As researchers investigating the effects of maternal employment have discovered, there are so many variables to consider—why a mother is working, how many hours she works, what kinds of help she gets, how old her children are, what types of child-care arrangements she makes, how supportive and enriching the child-care environment may be, to name just a few.[6] Also, as parents are apt to point out, raising children today is not just a question of attending to their physical needs, but also inculcating them with a set of values, values which are often personal and peculiar to a given family, particularly in such a pluralistic culture as ours. Parents raise their children not just to be one of a crowd, but to be special kinds of people, products of themselves. Yet it's too early even to expect a consensus of expert opinions on the issue of how much quality or quantity time is necessary for children to adopt much of the value system their parents wish to pass on. Besides, until we have a generation of children who were raised by employed mothers in turn raising their own children, how can we really know how this social experiment will turn out?

Even apart from these concerns about whether quality time is good for children, there has recently been an upsurge of interest in what women themselves get from mothering. When the majority of women were homemakers, it was perhaps most interesting and worthwhile to speculate on how much more satisfied they would be if freed from the demands of child rearing and domestic servitude. While mothers have by no means been released from these gender-assigned duties, now that the majority of women are in the labor force, speculation shifts to interest in what kinds of rewards women reap from mothering. That is, how much time spent child rearing is critical not for children, but for mothers? Do women feel they have enough time with their children if they devote long hours to work outside the home? Do they still gain the same satisfactions and have enough time, patience, and energy to experience the highs of parenting, its joys and pleasures?

It has now become more acceptable to question the merit of quality time. Some women who have established successful careers and reached the top in their fields have begun to wonder whether they missed out on something important by not being there when their children were young. At a conference at Wellesley College in the Spring of 1982, Jean Baker Miller, author of many books and articles on the psychology of women and practicing clinician, spoke of her regrets about never having saved enough time to enjoy her children.[7] How many women in the mainstream have ever stood behind the banner of quality time is unclear. What is evident, however, is that there is now a greater sense of openness and the potential for freer discussion among different groups of women. It is not only Phyllis Schlafly and the conservative fringe who are calling for reassessments of the importance of maternal child-rearing. Even some avowed feminists from the past are expressing a reluctance to continue riding on the quality-time bandwagon, perhaps as they have gained a greater appreciation for how maternal employment can change the dynamics and tensions of family life. (And perhaps, too, as they have realized that the workplace and male models of success provide no assurances of satisfaction and may be less rewarding than they were cracked up to be.) Is is humanly possible to have quality time when you come home tired and hungry after a hard day's work and then feel obligated not only to get dinner on the table and clean the house, but to listen attentively to what kind of day your oldest had at school and play with your two-year-old? To have the energy and patience to carry off such quality time, even when spouse and children pitch in to help, do mothers have to be Supermoms? Some old doubts which were never fully assuaged have also resurfaced. For example, does quality time rest upon a broad foundation of time spent together? Futhermore, is it reasonable to assume that children's needs and wants (and their willingness to talk and be with their parents, particularly as they grow older) will fit into the tight schedules which are often dictated when women add employment to family responsibilities? Will the child who wanted to discuss a problem at three o'clock be willing and able to still talk about it at eight?

Collectively, we seem unsure about whether quality time does work. Expert advice is of little help, since the experts themselves are so divided. One 1984 issue of *Esquire* magazine, purporting to be about the *New American Woman,* had back to back articles, both including quotes from highly regarded child development specialists, one approving of mothers working even when youngsters are very young and condoning the notion of quality time and the other stressing the importance of early mother–child interactions and the need to take time out of the labor force. No solution was presented to the dilemma many readers must face when confronted by such contrary expert opinion.[8] While some think it is all right for women to work even when they have infants, others talk of the importance of mothers being at home until children are two, three, five, or some other specific age. While some deem part-time jobs as acceptable, they disapprove of full-time positions which require longer periods away. And there are still others who remind us that it is not only young children who may need their mothers at home, but teenagers as well.[9]

How, then, have the women interviewed resolved the quality–quantity debate in their own minds? What do they think goes into being a good mother? It is to this topic that we now turn.

The Fleeting Years: A Special Time for Mothers and Children

It might be reasonable to expect that what comes next is a discussion which focuses on differences—on the stresses and tensions experienced by full-time homemakers versus those felt by mothers combining employment and child rearing, of the varied daily arrangements and lifestyles of women who have taken different paths, and so on. But the following is not so much about differences as it is about similarities. For the women who participated in this study may have entered motherhood with different understandings and expectations, but what is most striking about them is the extent to which they—followers, straddlers, and departers alike—now share a common understanding of what is important in their lives and what is important for their families. Older women as well as those with only high-school educations and few career expectations, those followers who by and large counted on being at home full-time, have found themselves increasingly pulled toward the world of employment, particularly as their children grow older. For example, over half (55 percent) of the followers were employed at the time of their interviews. Yet conversely, and perhaps more surprisingly, younger women, including those with college educations and professional training—the departers and straddlers—have found that the satisfactions they derive from child rearing and the demands of raising a family have moderated their views as well. Even as they experiment with combining paid work with domestic responsibilities, they have found themselves increasingly pulled toward home and family. The combined effects of these two pulls result in a rather striking consensus about what it means to be a mother today and about the limited, although special, nature of maternal employment.

By and large women were united in their rejection of the notion of quality time. They rejected it for what they perceived as two equally important reasons. First, because they continue to believe that children benefit from having their mothers available during both the routine and unpredictable happenings of daily life. Second, because in addition to feeling that children need them, mothers felt that they also need the time with their children. Woman after woman emphasized that children are only young for a short time and that during this special time it is mutually beneficial for mothers and children to be together as much as possible. In keeping with these beliefs, mothers rejected the notion that full-time employment is compatible with childrearing. Even of those women who were working full-time, less than a handful felt it was appropriate to take such a job when children were preschoolers. The majority of women felt full-time work interfered with family life even when school-age or teenage children were present. They based these conclusions both on their own experiences and on observations of other women they knew who have made different arrangements. In fact, most of the women presented their own views about what goes into being a good mother in juxtaposition to what they felt were oversights and misjudgments of others.

This is in part because in their interviews, mothers were encouraged to talk not only about themselves and their own mothering styles, but about the choices and lifestyles of other mothers. The purpose of such questioning was not to pit one woman against another unnecessarily nor to promote mere gossip, but to get beneath what seemed to be an almost knee-jerk and surface-level response. Most of the mothers wanted to present themselves as being tolerant, contemporary, and more often than not, somewhat "liberated." When first questioned about women's work and family roles, they, therefore, presented themselves as all accepting—it was fine for mothers to work at full-time, even high-pressure jobs; it was fine for mothers to be homemakers; it was fine for mothers to do just about whatever they wanted. However, as the women talked on in greater detail about their own choices and as they compared their lives and commitments to those of other women, they began making stronger value statements and grew more comfortable expressing some of the tensions and disapproval they apparently feel. Two questions were particularly useful for provoking the most unguarded discussions. The first was, Do you know someone who is doing things differently than you are—whether she is combining employment and child rearing or being a full-time homemaker—in a way you would not like for yourself or your own family? The second question posed a hypothetical situation. It asked respondents to imagine a friend had come to them for advice about whether she should get a job while her children were preschoolers. What would they tell her? Would their advice be different if her children were older, that is, either school-age or teenage? If necessary, after answering these two questions, women were asked to respond to some more general probes: Do you think there are things a mother can do for her family if she is home that she can't if she is working? What are the benefits if a mother is employed—for herself? for her family? Does a mother miss out on anything if she is employed? Does she gain anything if she stays home?

In examining their responses to this set of questions, it becomes evident that mothers have definite opinions about what goes into being a good mother. They feel strongly that there are better and worse ways to raise a family and integrate employment into one's life and they by no means approve of what they see everyone else doing. Through their comments, the boundaries of what they, and what we as a society, consider good mothering become clearer. Insights into how women in the mainstream define these boundaries, what types of behaviors and work–family decisions they see as overstepping the limits of being a good mother, and what kind of norms exist regarding the maternal role emerge from their collected statements.

Expectations Meet Reality

> I worked right up to the end of my pregnancy. But then when I had my son it was a whole new ball game. I didn't want to go back to work. In fact, I had promised my boss I would come back in less than a month for a couple of weeks' work. But I just couldn't stand not knowing who was taking care of Timothy. I mean, I knew my mother-in-law and my father-in-law would be there taking care of him and they were very capable, but, of course, they wouldn't do the job that I would do. And so I guess I was destined to be a mother.

Although this is certainly a strong statement about realizing one's destiny in motherhood, it does not necessarily follow that this woman was planning on being a full-time homemaker for the rest of her life. One recurring sentiment expressed by respondents was that only after giving birth did they come to learn how quickly children grow and how transitory the time is when they truly need full-time mothering. Women came to this understanding from two directions. Followers, who had expected to be at home for either most or the rest of their lives, discovered that the childhood years are fleeting and that the workplace beckons, both for reasons of personal fulfillment and because their growing families could use the extra income they could provide, particularly in these inflationary times. Although over one-third of the respondents reported that, on having their first baby, they never planned on going back to work, almost all had now come to realize that being home was, at most, only a temporary status. Only eight women planned on still being home in five years, and at least half of the eight had such plans because they expected to be tending to another infant. Of the remaining, two were currently working and felt that they would probably be looking forward to retiring or taking an extended vacation with their husbands at such a time. Employment was a significant factor in all the women's lives; not only were the majority working, but even those who weren't had started to plan what kind of jobs they would get in the future, when their days of full-time mothering came to an end.

The movement of women with more traditional expectations toward employment makes sense. As demographers point out, the combination of increased longevity coupled with decreasing fertility means women are child rearers for a smaller percentage of their lives now than in the past.[10] However, the growing awareness that child rearing only takes up a part of one's life also has implications for women who had planned on more continuous workplace involvement, the departers and some straddlers. These women spoke of how, as a result of the growing bond they felt with their children, they had begun to reconsider their priorities. Like the followers, these women came to think in different terms than they did before they became mothers. Their interviews are filled with such phrases as "they're only young for such a short time," "these early years are so fleeting," "they're only young once," phrases which echoed the sentiments of the older and less career-oriented women. As Helen Trilling, who worked off and on at part-time jobs starting when her eldest child was six months old, explained:

> I think a working mother does miss out on things. Especially when her children are really small. I missed out on a great deal of Greg's babyhood and I can see that my friend who is working and has a small child misses out on a great deal of her child's infancy, too. There's no other time in a child's life when they are growing so quickly and doing so many things. So I think that working mothers do miss out. But they miss out when their children are older also. When children come home from school and they have something to talk about, they want to talk about it now, and sometimes they don't remember after dinner. I have to remind them to tell their father about things that have happened that they told me about after school. If there is no one there to remind them, they forget. And you, as a mother, miss out on an awful lot.

Amanda Brown, the mother of two preschoolers and a former librarian, reiterated these points:

> I think it's really important to be at home with your kids. They're only going to be little for such a short time. It's just so fleeting and I really am appreciating them so much more every day.... These moments are just not going to come again no matter how many pictures you take. I just think that people who leave their kids are losing a lot. I think that input is so important, the one-on-one relationship, day after day. You read all these articles about quality time, but I just can't quite see it. I think it's that always being around for every little problem, all day long—it adds up. I think that's what is important in a relationship.

Seeing how quickly children grow (and how pleasurable it can be to watch them change and develop), such women had cut back on their plans for employment. They delayed their plans to return to work shortly after a baby's birth and they often reversed their preparenthood decisions to try balancing full-time employment with child rearing.

It is possible to make the argument that women are pulled toward child rearing because of the absence of available child care alternatives or similar supports which would ease an employed mother's work load. There is some truth to this; for example, fathers were generally unavailable during daylight hours and while women felt their husbands were the most appropriate substitutes for maternal care, few couples had the option to share more fully in daily child rearing chores. However, there is more to women's decisions to stay home or limit work hours than the lack of other viable options. For rather than emphasizing what children need from their mothers, women also stressed the importance of being there because of the satisfactions mothers derive from close contact with their children. Women who had thought it would be easy to go to work and leave their youngsters in someone else's care were most surprised by the strength of their desire to be more involved in child rearing. Women who identified closely with the women's movement and who advocated women's advancement in the ranks of the employed had to reconcile their new feelings about mothering with their more work-oriented ideologies. In doing so, they tended to deemphasize the importance of full-time maternal care for children but to highlight what mothers gain from taking some time off work. As one mother, typical of the departers described:

> I believe that a woman can combine both working and raising kids and do whatever she wants to do, if she wants to badly enough.... So I don't say any mother who doesn't stay home with her children is cheating them or anything like that. I just think she is cheating herself. I think it's just nice to be with them all the time and see them when they stumble or fall. And hold them when they cry. There's all those more spontaneous types of things a mother would miss out on if she were working.

Similarly, although departer Natalie Green was interviewed at a turning point in her life, when she was feeling she would like to return to work to gain more intellectual satisfaction and to make use of her job skills, she also stressed how important it had been for her to stay home while her daughter was a preschooler and how hard life would have been for everyone in her family, including herself, if she was working:

> There are just a lot of wonderful little moments that you share when you're there. My husband and I call them *Golden Moments—GMs*. They're things that you can't really think about or plan for—like [all of a sudden her saying] "Oh, Mommy, I love you!" Those moments you have together when you're not necessarily under stress. You might miss those if you work eight or ten hours and then come home and are fixing dinner. You're always under an

added stress if you're working. For example, dinner time even under the best of circumstances is stressful.... Kids are very, very tired that time of day and they want your attention. You're trying to get dinner ready and your husband comes in and he's also tired and wants to talk a little bit. It's a time when you wouldn't mind someone giving to you, but you really have to do all the giving. And if you're just coming home from work yourself at that time, you're just in a position to take and not to give.

There's Never a Perfect Solution: Ambivalence and Transitions

When she was interviewed, Jan Lesser was working as a secretary twenty-four hours a week. She felt she was one of the fortunate few—her hours were flexible, her boss was understanding, she could take vacations and summers off—whose job did not cut deeply into the time she spent with her family.

> I know when my daughter was first born I loved going to work. But when I was at work, sometimes I would think "What is she doing now at home? I'm not there." Even though my mom was here, and I knew she'd take care of her. You always have that feeling you'll miss out on something. And yet when you're home, you always feel you could be doing something or working at this point.... It's nice to go back to work if everything works out; but, then, if it doesn't work out, it's a complete flop.

While the overwhelming majority of women had decided to stay home for a time when children were young or to limit their employment (this was the case for almost 95 percent of the respondents), this does not mean that they experienced few misgivings or little ambivalence about their arrangements. To be sure, those women who always had expected to spend a large portion of their lives devoted to full-time mothering expressed few doubts about their time at home. However, for those who came to motherhood expecting it to have little impact on their workplace involvements, it was often more difficult to reconcile the demands and pulls of child rearing with prior goals. When children were very young, feelings of doubt and ambivalence were often submerged in the midst of hectic schedules and fairly constant reminders of being needed. As children approached school-age, however, the reasons to stay at home became less clear for many women, and this is the time when concerns about the future began to surface. For example, Natalie Green worked for over ten years as a medical research technician before becoming a mother. With her daughter now five years old, she is torn between continuing to stay at home or trying to reestablish her career. She doesn't really want to settle for a part-time, dead-end job (as she sees many of her friends doing), but she isn't sure what she should be doing. As she explained:

> I had no real idea of what motherhood was until I had a child. You just don't. It's intangible, that's what I'd like to say. I can't really put into words what

motherhood is. There is just an indescribable bond that exists and I'm very, very glad that I stayed home with Sarah these years. I really enjoyed doing things with her, being with her. But I need more now and it's very difficult to combine it. If I were to work a full-time job now, I am quite aware of the havoc it would create here. And I haven't put it together so as to how I can get my own intellectual satisfaction and do for my family what I want to do.

Several other women, also at transition points in their lives, expressed similar sentiments. Yet even in the midst of their uncertainty about the best course for the future, they took pains to explain that they did not regret the time they had devoted to child rearing. "I'm glad I've done things the way I have," explained one mother, "but now I have to figure out what to do next." The sense of control which permeates such a statement is obvious, as is the lack of regret. Perhaps as they see more and more of their friends reentering the labor force after time at home, it becomes easier for women to see their lives as a series of transitions—a time for full-time employment, a time to be at home or to limit work hours, followed by a time to be full-time employed again. As was evident in a few cases (particularly when women had been home for upwards of ten years), these transition points can be difficult and they can force an individual to reassess her goals and life ambitions. For most women, however, they were taken as a natural part of the life course.

Despite considerable variation in how long a period of time women advocated being full-time mothers—whether they saw this phase as lasting ten, fifteen, or twenty or more years, or whether they saw it only as a brief interlude—there was general agreement about why some time at home was crucial, if not for the sake of children, then for the sake of mothers. As Jill Lucey would advise a friend who was considering taking a paid job:

> I would tell her to try and hold off for as long as she could, like until the kids were in school and they're gone an appreciable amount of time. Then she would still be taking most of the responsibility for her children and not leaving it to a babysitter. . . . I think that children are only loaned to you. . . . You only have them a really short time, and you never really know how long. We have a friend whose youngster just died and that's reinforced my feeling that you just don't know how long you have them. This particular mother is having a guilt trip because as soon as the baby was born she zipped back to work and now she has this terrible, tremendous guilt. She should have been home since she no longer has him.

Most women were not so melodramatic in describing how they cherished the time spent with their children, but they too placed an emphasis on how important it was to have some uncommitted space, to enjoy children and witness their successes and falls without employment infringing and imposing time limits and constraints. Coming to a shared understanding, respondents—followers, straddlers, and departers—expressed the feeling that just as children are only young once, the time mothers need to devote to child rearing is also transitory. The women were almost unanimous in warning others not to miss out on these special years, even though it may mean cutting back on workplace involvements and redefining one's career goals.

How Much Time Is Enough?

One phrase repeated throughout many interviews was: "I don't understand why people have children if they don't want to spend time with them." These words were used not just by the few women who were most adamant about children needing full-time mothers. On the contrary, this or a similar phrase occurred in fully a third of the interviews with women who were working at part-time or even full-time jobs themselves, as well as in most of the interviews with full-time homemakers. There was a definite outside limit on how much time was deemed acceptable for mothers to be away from their children. Full-time work, particularly when children were preschoolers and often beyond through their teenage years, was not only viewed as unadvisable (unless, of course, it was a financial necessity), but was often treated with considerable consternation. Of the twelve women who worked full-time, only two still had preschool children. Both of these women, moreover, were teachers, with hours that enabled them to be home both early in the afternoon and during lengthy summer and school vacations (four of the full-time workers with school-age children were teachers with similar work schedules). Three additional full-time workers were single parents, with no other option than to work and one was a woman who openly admitted her marriage was in jeopardy and was preparing for the possibility of a future on her own. Of the remaining two, one woman was a service-worker with flexible hours and the other was an administrator at a local hospital. Only the administrator was away from home more than eight hours a day for a full year—and her only child was going to celebrate his twelfth birthday in a few months. For most of the past twelve years, she had been a full-time homemaker.

Respondents had strong reservations about women combining full-time employment with child rearing. Mothers who opted for full-time employment were portrayed as neglectful, or even worse, as selfish. They were viewed as placing their own needs above the needs of their family. While no one advocated women being selfless and ever-giving (and no one argued that women should be able to derive all their satisfaction and fulfillment from their families), full-time employees were at times censured for placing their own desires first and the needs of their children and spouses, second. As one woman with a part-time job recounted:

> I think it can be a sacrifice [for women to stay home], and I feel that a lot of women don't want to make that sacrifice. It is the "me" generation. That's

good, because I think you have to have some things for me. You can't be sacrificing all the time. . . . But it's almost as though some women want their careers, they want to be married, and they want to have that child, too. They must think, "before I lose out, I've got to have that child; I want that experience as well." Then they just leave the child and they go off to work. I've even heard this story where one woman's husband wanted a child and she didn't want one as much. So she agreed to have a child, just that one child, and then she would go right back to work. I wonder why people have children, then. Is it just to say you have a child? I mean, why have them if you don't want to be with them?

There was a virtual consensus of opinion regarding the unadvisability of full-time employment. As a result, women professionals—the group seen as most likely to be working full-time out of choice—were dealt with harshly. The following examples demonstrate this bias against career women and are illustrative of where women in the mainstream draw the line between what they consider good mothering and a mother's excessive employment commitment. Jessica Matthews, the mother of a four-year-old son and a ten-year-old daughter, had worked off and on since her children were very young—but always at part-time jobs when her husband was available for child care:

It's funny you're asking me about women working, because I just got offered a job. The girl next door just had a baby. The baby is six weeks old and she has a good job coming up in the fall and she has asked me to take the baby every day from eight to six. Her reasoning is that she has priorities and the baby is second in priorities; her job is first. I just couldn't understand it. I just told her, "for me to take your baby all those hours of the day, it would be like bringing up my own child. And I would become very attached to it, and I would be bringing it up as my own, basically." I felt as though that's her responsibility. She should be the one doing this, especially during the formative years.

Lois Carr had worked part-time for most of the time since her second child was born. However, she never needed to make regular child-care arrangements since she limited her work hours so that they matched those hours her husband was home or her children were in school. On occasion, her two girls played at friends' houses for a few hours after school until she returned from work.

I have difficulty with people I know who work full-time and have children. Maybe I'm just in-between generations, but I can't understand why they have children if they work full-time. To me, it seems like if they're not home, why bother to have kids? I could never do that in a million years. . . . Plus there are times that I feel guilty when I do work and I can't imagine the guilt it must take to leave a baby at home. . . . I just think it's really important that a mother is here and ready to listen to them and help them sort out their problems. It's the security. I just can't imagine the kids coming home to a babysitter or even a grandparent.

Joan Levine, a former school teacher, was working about thirty hours a week as an administrative assistant at the time she was interviewed. Her work hours coincided with the school day. When her children were preschoolers, she tutored other youngsters in her home.

> I really feel that the first five years are the formative years of a child's life and even though the saying is today that quality time is more important than quantity time, I can't see someone coming home at six o'clock at night and spending two hours with a child when someone else has been there to kiss their boo-boo and take them to the park and watch them take their first step. I just don't see how you can build a relationship with someone on one or two hours a day. I just don't see how that's done and I also feel that children do not ask to be brought into this world. That is the choice of the parents. And I think that the child should come first rather than you as a parent.

Marian Farina waited until her children wer all in school and then landed a highly sought-after job as a secretary for the school department in her community. She worked only school hours, and had summers and all school vacations off.

> I don't like to approve or disapprove, but I'm not too fond of seeing two professionals working and leaving their children with a babysitter. I've seen it in my own neighborhood. What often happens is there's a change of babysitters. Then once the children are old enough, whether it's nursery-school age or whatever, they're sent off to schools and camps. I really feel as though the children aren't learning one set of values. They're really learning the babysitter's sense of values. and their babysitters keep changing.

Even women who held what could technically be considered full-time jobs spoke of the need to moderate work schedules while children were young. Such women distinguished their employment (usually as teachers or nurses with limited or flexible hours) from what they considered real full-time employment, that is, the types of work schedules that are demanded of women doctors, lawyers, and the like. For example, Deborah Hartman had resumed a part-time teaching load the fall after her son was born. She recently increased her hours to full-time. However, either she or her husband, who taught in the same school, made sure to be home by two-thirty each work day, before their son walked in the door after school. Employment meant more to her than it did to almost any other woman interviewed, but she too cautioned against what she perceived as an excessive work commitment:

> I would encourage another mother to work but I would make it clear that, for me, work has been really important—for her it might not be. I don't think that I would say, "you are a bad person, you are weak and incompetent if you can't work." But I would encourage her not to feel any guilt and to realize that there

is time. But I think full-time work is really—well, I have reservations about that. My sister-in-law and her husband have two small children and they both work from seven-thirty in the morning to seven at night and they have a live-in woman. I think that's absurd. Why have children? Why go through the aggravation if you can't have an impact on them, on their lives and values? I don't think you can do that in the hour you get them ready for bed. Nobody can. I want to have a role in my children's lives, and I feel that I want my husband to have a role. . . . And so, I would encourage a part-time situation. I know that's not possible for everyone, but I would think that's the best.

The Importance of Being There

Why did women feel it is so important for mothers to be there with children, to be their primary caretakers? There are two reasons, really, but both are intricately entwined. First, by virtue of being there, it was generally assumed that mothers could maintain a certain level of control over their children and thus pass on to them those values and ways of life which are important to them. Beyond meeting children's social, emotional, and intellectual needs, the women emphasized the importance of being there to guide children's outlooks and morals. Although research on the effects of maternal employment on children has not looked at this aspect of child rearing, it is evident that mothers consider it one of the foremost tasks of parenting. Joan O'Hara, the mother of four who has worked most of the last two years, summed up the feelings of many others:

> It's just the idea that you're here and if there is any disciplining to be done or any bruise to take care of, you can do it your way. If you don't want them to make a big issue of it, you can make light of it. It's mostly a way of life that you're giving your children. You're bringing them up to be future citizens. Especially during the preschool years—the formative years; the ideas that are formed then can't be changed later. . . . Basically, I think it is easier to say yes to a child for the time being and give him the cookie or the toy he's looking for and get him out of your hair. And if someone else is taking care of your children, they're not necessarily going to have your children's best interests at heart. Just like a grandmother comes and she brings a treat for the children. It's her way of winning them over, but it isn't necessarily what you always want.

As a number of women with older children pointed out, the need for such parental guidance doesn't necessarily end when children are school-age or even older. At times, it even increases. Several women had tried full-time jobs only to discover their teenagers had "started to do things we didn't like or approve of." They then cut back their work hours or decided to return to being full-time homemakers, at least for a while longer. Being there for children, being on hand to monitor what they do and to pass on a set of values, was seen as crucial. It was one of the most basic criteria of being a good mother and one of the highest priorities of women at this life stage.

The second reason women stressed the importance of being there is related to the issue of passing on values and a way of life, but entails a change of perspective. For in being there to share those golden moments, to guide and support children through their big and small crises, mothers portrayed that they also came out as winners. While some lamented that for the considerable number of hours and years they spent child rearing they had received no paychecks and garnered no formal recommendations or recognition, they were filled with pride for their children and for the adults they felt their children would one day become. Despite many well-documented drawbacks (such as days spent without adult conversation), motherhood was seen as having its own rewards, rewards which most of the women felt have been discounted or disregarded for too long. How awful it would be, a number of women suggested, to pick up your child at a day-care center or at a babysitter's house after a day of work and have them not want to come home. Even worse yet, few could imagine anything more horrible than hearing your own child call someone else "Mommy"—yet they felt such things can, and do, happen if mothers cross the critical boundary between being there and spending too much time away from their homes and child rearing. After relating such a story yet again, one woman ended her discussion with the often repeated refrain, "Why bother to have children if you don't want to be there; really, what is the point?"

Eliminating the Alternatives

In listening to the women's statements, it becomes apparent that this generation's reservations about full-time work and mothers maintaining professional careers could not be overcome completely through the provision of more, or even better, child-care facilities. Concerns and fears about alternative child-care arrangements go far deeper. They center more around whether nonmaternal child care is an acceptable choice at all than on whether there are accessible and affordable child-care facilities. Only seven women agreed that it was all right to leave preschoolers with babysitters or in day-care centers. Not surprisingly, these were the same seven women who had made such arrangements in the past, at the time when they took their first jobs after becoming mothers. It was far more common for women to delay returning to work until children were established either in nursery- or elementary-school programs. Nursery schools, with their aura of middle-class respectability, provided child-care relief for both employed and nonemployed mothers, yet because they were perceived primarily as educational institutions and only secondarily as child care, they did not carry with them the same stigma as arranging for babysitters or day care.

At the time of the interviews, only one child was enrolled in a day-care center. While the child's mother was very pleased with the setting, particularly since it allowed her to attend law school, a neighbor who (by chance) was also interviewed spoke disparagingly about the family's misguided priorities and use of what she felt was an inappropriate substitute for maternal care. Only two families had regularly scheduled arrangements with private babysitters. On the whole, children were either in school the entire time their mother worked (as was the case in 58 percent of the families where mothers were employed), taken care of by relatives (9 percent), or involved in some composite of less formal arrangements, such as having children alternate their time between after-school enrichment programs and playing with friends at their houses (30 percent or 13 families). For the most part, when they were not in school, children were in the care of their mothers.[11]

Because mothers placed such a high priority on being around when children were home, they simply did not feel any great need for child care. While some respondents advocated the creation of more quality child-care facilities for mothers who truly needed them, they themselves most often structured their own lives so as not to be forced to rely upon such services. (In other words, they may be necessary and good enough for some families—but not for their own.) Even when others were not actually condemned for using day-care centers or babysitters, such arrangements were, at best, only condoned. A few women related situations where they thought children were actually better off without their mothers. As Ellen Muise reported:

> I know someone that has a little boy who has been in child care since he was two. She just never should have had this little boy!...He got very good care there but it works and it doesn't work. I think his mother was very selfish so probably they are better off being separated. It's better that she isn't home with him because she had no affection or patience with this baby at all. He had been to day care and day camp and this last year he was in kindergarten. His father works for himself, so he was kind of dragged around from one job to another with his father or dropped off with the woman down the street to be taken care of in the afternoon after kindergarten.

Single parents, viewed as victims of their circumstances, were excused if they had to place their children in the care of others. Women who opted for such arrangements, when they technically had the opportunity to spend more time with their offspring, were not. Yet there was the feeling that certain women were not cut out to be mothers. Bored at home, they would begin to take it out on their children. In these cases, children were seen as just as well off being raised by others. For the majority of women who tried to live up to a certain image of good mothering, however, such options were rarely considered seriously.

The Role of Fathers

Fathers were deemed the best substitute for maternal care, yet few men were able to take enough time off their jobs to be counted on for substantial help with children. Social-class differences were apparent in how much fathers did help out. In Claremont, where more men had blue-collar and nonprofessional jobs, it was somewhat more common for couples at one time or another to have worked split shifts, with one parent arriving home before the other went off to work (eleven of the fifteen couples who had made such arrangements lived in Claremont). However, only couples with certain kinds of jobs could rely on such schedules. In more affluent Green Haven, men were more likely to have higher status jobs which required that they put in long, and often erratic, hours at work; they could not be counted on to come home every day by three-thirty in order to participate in a change of child-care shifts. In addition, mothers in Green Haven were less likely to have the types of jobs where it is possible to work nights and evenings; they did not work as waitresses, nurses' aides, and so on, as did many of the women in Claremont.

For the most part, both in Green Haven and in Claremont, fathers were viewed primarily as breadwinners. Just one father had taken time off work in order to provide substantial hours of child care. While fathers were expected to be there to provide some relief on evenings and weekends as well as to join in shared family times, they were not relied upon as major sources of child care. Few wives reported they were displeased with this division of labor. They saw their husbands working hard, and, often times, operating under a good deal of stress. Valerie K. Oppenheimer has written of the male "family-cycle squeeze" —men are called upon to earn more money and climb the ladder of success at the same time they have young children at home.[12] Most women saw their husbands as caught in this squeeze and thus felt it would be unfair to ask them to take on more responsibility for the house and children.

Husbands were responsible for bringing home most of the family income (remember that, on the whole, the women we interviewed had stable marriages and husbands who were stably employed). In only twelve cases did wives bring home more than $10,000 per year; no husbands earned less and almost all earned at least twice and sometimes even three or four times as much. The disproportionate earnings of husbands and wives tended to lock families into fairly traditional patterns. Husbands who were perceived as working hard at their paid jobs were released from many household chores and child-rearing responsibilities. In turn, the less a woman made in comparison to her spouse, the more she was likely to portray her paid job as a luxury, as something she was doing solely for her own personal fulfillment. This was the case even in a number of those families where mothers were working at full-time, professional (for example, teaching) jobs. The husbands of these women had even higher-paying, higher-status positions; husbands' employment thus diminished some of the importance and value of their wives' jobs. Because of this imbalance, many women did not even expect their husbands to do additional work around the house if and when they added employment to their jobs as mothers. (For a few, this was a sufficient deterrent to keep them from looking for paid jobs.) While they ideally would have liked their husbands to chip in more around the house, they felt it would be unreasonable to ask anything else of them. Conversely, the more a woman's salary was depended upon to bolster the family income, the more husbands were likely to increase their help around the house once their wives went to work. Accordingly, almost half of the men in more working-class Claremont increased the time they spent attending to child care and domestic chores when their wives entered the labor force (eleven out of twenty-six, or 42 percent of the women in Claremont who have been employed reported their husbands increased their unpaid family work; only 20 percent of the fathers in Green Haven did so.)

In general, fathers in Claremont played a greater role in day-to-day child care; they tended to spend less hours at work and a greater number of hours at home than the more career-oriented fathers in Green Haven (except for a couple of Claremont fathers who worked at two jobs). One woman who recently moved to Green Haven was shocked at how much time most fathers in the community spent at work. She felt her husband was one of the only men who came home regularly every day by four o'clock. Although such behavior was not unusual in the working-class community where they used to live, not one of the other fathers on her new block was home so early. Many of the children in Green Haven didn't see their fathers until six or seven at night, yet her husband was out playing ball with the neighborhood kids in the afternoon, and their family dinner was on the table at five. Such a schedule would not seem that unusual or out of place in Claremont, but in Green Haven, it was almost unheard of. Fathers were typically gone long hours every workday, and often worked on weekends as well.

Despite these differences, however, the division of labor between husbands and wives in both communities was pretty clear-cut. Most husbands "helped out" with child care and the house on occasion (usually when asked), and many wives "helped out" by bringing home some additional family income. Fathers were primary breadwinners and mothers were the primary child-care providers. Even women with high levels of education and avowedly more liberated ideas acknowledged that this was simply the way the world works. For example, they pointed out that they would be hard pressed to reverse roles and become responsible for bringing home as much money as their husbands.

The surprise is not that this is how the world still works for women in the mainstream of the United States—all one has to do is spend an afternoon walking around the streets and parks in Claremont, Green Haven, or any similar type of community where working- and middle-class couples raise their children to realize women still retain the bulk of child-rearing responsibilities. A handful of men may get the opportunity to spend a summer day at the town pool with their youngsters, but it is mothers and children who continue to dominate the scene. What is surprising, however, is the extent to which mothers not only accept this situation, but actually appear to enjoy it. To be sure, most would prefer that their husbands were more available, but few—very few—would want to give up much more of the time they have to spend with their families. Based on the evidence obtained from these mothers, it's not reasonable to explain their continuing commitments to child rearing merely in terms of constraints, the lack of child-care alternatives, the lack of good jobs for women, or male domination. Rather, women are pulled to their children not just because of what youngsters need from them but also because of the rewards and satisfactions adults can reap from being intimately involved in the nurturance and development of a younger generation. Perhaps it is only as women have gained the opportunity to be more than just mothers, as they realize they can incorporate other forms of meaningful employment into their lives before, after, and even during the time they raise children, that the benefits of mothering become truly evident. The years women spend as child rearers can no longer be viewed as the only productive ones of their lives. But this does not mean they are not among the most rewarding and personally satisfying.

Notes

1. This argument about maternal employment was first made in Lydia O'Donnell and Ann Stueve, "Mothers as Social Agents: Structuring the Community Activities of School-Age Children."

2. George Masnick and Mary Jo Bane, *The Nation's Families.*

3. Benjamin Spock has considerably revised his child-care manual over the years, starting out by assuming the importance of full-time mothering (and the fact that most women would be at home) and growing to appreciate mothers' work outside the home and fathers' involvements in child care. Compare, for example, two editions of *Baby and Child Care,* the first published by Meredith Books, New York, 1968, and the other by Pocket Books, New York, 1976. An impressive number of changes have been made in less than a ten-year period.

4. Feminists advocating ways out of the child-care bind have unfortunately too often neglected or underplayed cultural differences in child-rearing attitudes and values, as when they suggest that one way of solving mothers' problems in our country would be to adopt more communal child-rearing arrangements, group houses, communal cooking facilities, and so on. See, for example, Jesse Bernard's chapter on "Adjusting the Establishment to the Lives of Women," in her book, *Women in the Public Interest,* Chicago: Aldine–Atherton, 1971. Such solutions have apparently not been acceptable to the majority of U.S. families or women.

5. Selma Fraiberg, *Every Child's Birthright: In Defense of Mothering,* New York: Basic Books, 1978.

6. There has been a rapidly expanding body of literature on the effects of maternal employment on children. One frequently referred to review of the literature is Lois W. Hoffman, "Effects of Maternal Employment on the Child—A Review of the Research," *Developmental Psychology* 10, 1974, 104–228. Also see Joanne Curry O'Connell, "Children of Working Mothers: What the Research Tells Us," *Young Children,* January 1983, 62–73.

7. Jean Baker Miller, Director of the Stone Center for Developmental Research at Wellesley College, made these comments in a conference to alumnae at Wellesley College, Spring 1982.

8. The two articles are Harry Stein, "The Case for Staying Home" and Terri Minsky, "Advice and Comfort for the Working Mother" in *A Celebration of the New American Woman,* Special Issue of *Esquire,* June 1984, 142–161.

9. Child rearing how-to books have been popular for well over a century, but have appeared on the scene in increasing numbers over the past several decades. For different approaches to discussing women's roles, see Fitzhugh Dodson, *How to Parent,* New York: NAL, 1970; Letty Cottin Pogrebin, *Growing Up Free,* New York: McGraw Hill, 1980; Benjamin Spock, *Baby and Child Care;* Burton White, *The First Three Years,* to name just a few.

10. Mary Jo Bane, *Here to Stay.*

11. For further information on the child-care arrangements of working parents nationwide, see Mary Jo Bane, Laura Lein, Lydia O'Donnell, Ann Stueve, and Barbara Welles, "Child Care Arrangements of Working Parents," *Monthly Labor Review* 102, October 1979, 50–55.

12. Valerie K. Oppenheimer, "The Male-Family Cycle Squeeze: The Interaction of Men's Occupational and Family Life Cycle," *Demography* 11, May 1974, 227–245.

6
Employment Options and Rewards

W e have thus far seen how vital women feel it is to be there for children and how much they perceive both youngsters and mothers gaining from time spent together. Given the limits imposed by their commitments to child rearing, the question then becomes, why are so many employed? Moreover, why do so many feel that employment has become a crucial part of their lives? What do mothers think they gain from involvement in the labor force and why are there so many women who would actually prefer to combine paid (although typically part-time) jobs with their family work? In short, how is it possible that women highlight their responsibility to mothering at the same time they relate the importance of a woman's work away from home?

Respondents, regardless of whether they were employed and irrespective of such factors as their age, level of education, or prior expectations of how they would combine child rearing and paid jobs, shared an appreciation of the reasons why mothers take paid jobs. Three main reasons for, and benefits of, employment were evident. First, women agreed that employed mothers gain the opportunity to bolster the family income at the same time they experience the personal gratification which comes from bringing home a paycheck. Second, they acknowledged that paid jobs provide an opportunity for personal fulfillment and achievement in an arena outside the home and family. Finally, they felt that the workplace generally offers a woman the chance to interact with other adults and to engage in conversations on topics other than child rearing and domestic life. That women recognized these potential benefits of employment, however, did not mean they were necessarily employed or looking for work. Whether an individual saw any of these as sufficiently compelling to pull her into the labor force was dependent on a number of factors: how much she could count on her spouse for financial support and how high an income she deemed necessary to maintain what she considered an acceptable quality of life; what kinds of expectations and aspirations she held regarding jobs and a career; how long she had already been home with her children and how much time she felt it was necessary to spend in full-time child rearing.

Not surprisingly, there were notable differences between women who were employed and those who were not. For example, women who were younger (below the median age of thirty-seven) and better educated than the sample as a whole were more likely to be working, particularly full-time. Eight of the twelve (or 67 percent) full-time employees were college graduates, compared with only 44 percent of the total sample. In addition, such women tended to spend less time out of the labor force around the births of their children. Whereas over 50 percent of the women under the age of thirty-seven had gone back to work before their youngest child was three, this was a path followed by less than one in three of the older women. Thus, a woman's age and her level of education influenced not only her expectations of how long she would be at home, but her actual work patterns as well. In addition, a woman's family stage (that is, the age of her youngest child) played a significant role in determining when she would look for a paid job. Sixty percent of those women with a child under the age of six were full-time homemakers, 32 percent were employed part-time, and only 8 percent (or two women) had full-time jobs. In contrast, only one-third of the women with children six and older remained full-time homemakers, almost half had part-time jobs, and 20 percent were employed full-time. (An employment profile of the women is presented in table 6–1.)

Paid Work as a Source of Income

Certainly the single most influential factor in determining whether a woman was working was how much her family counted on her income to get by. About 10 percent of the mothers had no other choice but to work; either they were single parents and primary breadwinners or their husbands were ill or for some other reason unable to support a family on their own. Having little or no choice, such women often felt trapped by the dual demands of child rearing and paid work. While they were aware that employment has some inherent benefits, they tended to highlight its difficulties and personal costs. For example, Sara Cherkersian, a single mother with two school-age sons, spent a considerable portion of her interview talking about the things she was no longer able to do now that she was employed full-time. As she saw it, her time and energy were so constrained that it was almost impossible to get even the basic household chores accomplished, much less than to spend some special, quality time with her children before bed. She complained about how tired and hassled she was by the end of each day. In her closing comments, she summarized her feelings:

> I don't think that society is very sympathetic to women like me, even though there are a lot more single women out there today. Because people think we're

Table 6-1
Employment Profile of Mothers

Current Employment Status (at time of interviews)		
At Home	42%	(31)
Part-time Employed (up to 34 hours/week)	42%	(31)
Full-time Employed	16%	(12)
Number of Hours Employed Women Worked per Week[a]		
Less than 10 Hours	12%	(5)
11–20	35%	(15)
21–29	19%	(8)
30–34	7%	(3)
35 and Over	28%	(12)
Type of Current Job		
Professional/Technical	20%	(15)
Managers/Administrators	5%	(4)
Clerical	24%	(18)
Other (including sales, service, factory)	8%	(6)
Homemaking	42%	(31)

[a] $n = 43$.

having a great time being liberated women working at jobs. But all the pressures are just doubled. It's having full responsibility for the kids after coming home from a full day of work.

Likewise, other women in similarly constrained situations spoke of how they were employed "just to make money." Ann McGuinn, who was forced to take on full-time work when her husband suffered a heart attack, made a point of emphasizing that she was working solely because her family counted on her income. She saw few other benefits of her job, not even the opportunity it provided her to get out of the house. As she explained:

I was getting out plenty before I had to take my job.... I wasn't bored being at home. When your kids are older you can get involved with different clubs and all. I mean, I had quite a nice little social life. But I couldn't afford to stay home.

What distinguishes followers like Sara Cherkersian and Ann McGuinn is that they hadn't expected to be working at this point in their lives, especially not at the types of full-time jobs they were forced to take. They had both counted on more years as full-time homemakers, yet the vagaries of fate had forced them into paid jobs. While they recognized that as their children got older they might have been looking around for other things to do (even under the best of circumstances), they had envisioned lives of part-time work, volunteering, or some other less pressured arrangements. They had not counted on working while they were raising children and, although they were managing quite well by most objective standards, they by no means advocated others following their footsteps.

There were several other women who were in similar situations where they were compelled to work. While employment was more compatible with their expectations and did not come as quite as big a surprise, they also tended to speak in terms of constraints and how they felt boxed in by the joint demands of children and work. For example, one woman, a college-educated fashion designer and single parent, was torn: any position which would both bring in enough money to support herself and her son as well as provide intellectual and career fulfillment would also require a great many hours on the job and perhaps even necessitate a move to another state, alternatives she dismissed since she did not feel they were in the best interests of her family. As a result, she opted for part-time work locally and tried to supplement her income by doing freelance consulting wherever and whenever she could get the work. She was thus able to spend time with her son and avoid moving him away from the rest of his family and friends—but at considerable cost. She was having trouble making ends meet financially and she was getting little personal satisfaction from her work. At best, she saw herself making a compromise; at worse, she thought of herself as trapped in an irreconcilable situation.

It is hardly a new discovery that single parents are overburdened. Many of the married women interviewed were awed by the amount of work expected of women in such circumstances. "I just don't know how she manages to get everything done and still hold things together," one woman said of her neighbor, a single mother. Yet single mothers themselves had little energy to be self-congratulatory or to derive much satisfaction from their efforts. Often, they felt they were losing at both ends. They cut back on their work hours as much as possible so as to conserve family time, yet in doing so they often sacrificed many of the pleasures of employment, such as jobs with career potential, time to socialize with friends at the workplace, and so on. Similarly, despite their efforts to limit employment, they found themselves cutting corners at home as well. Without the luxury of choice, employment was experienced more as a hardship than as a source of satisfaction and rewards.

Employment as an Option: Supplementing the Family Income

Most of the respondents residing in Green Haven and Claremont had more choice over whether and how much to work than the women described above.

They were married and their husbands made relatively good salaries. Yet even in the majority of these cases, family income was a determining factor in whether a woman sought a paid job. There are a number of ways this point can be illustrated. For example, only three women who lived on family incomes of less than $20,000 per year were full-time homemakers. Moreover, families with homemakers had the same modal income as did families where mothers were employed (between $20,000 and $30,000 per year). What this suggests is that by virtue of their paid work, women brought their family income up to a fairly standard level, on par with the amount for families with full-time homemakers. In both communities, there was general agreement that it took at least $20,000 to $30,000 a year to get by (with Claremont families clustering on the low end and Green Haven residents on the upper limit). If husbands earned this amount on their own, it was less likely that their wives would seek employment; when husbands' incomes were less than this amount, wives' salaries were counted on to boost family income to an acceptable and socially normative level. This means that families with employed mothers were not necessarily better off than families dependent only on husbands' incomes. In fact, the few most affluent families tended to be those with full-time homemakers. Full-time homemaking was indeed cast as a luxury, an option that many, if not most women, do not have. Mothers worked as a way of keeping up with the Joneses rather than as a way of getting ahead.

There were those, however, who perceived maternal employment in different terms, in a way that is illustrative of the tension which exists between groups of women who have made different choices. Some non-employed women, followers who emphasized the importance of full-time mothering, felt that many of the mothers they saw working were doing so not for essentials, but to buy their families luxuries and often superfluous extras, such as trips to Disneyworld and the latest fashion clothes. In that they felt they were doing without such luxuries in order to act upon their commitment to full-time mothering, they felt many women who opted for employment had made a poor tradeoff between gaining an extra income and being there for their children; their criticisms were tinged with some resentment.

How much income is truly necessary is, of course, difficult to answer since it is mostly a matter of personal interpretation and lifestyle. Simply, one family's essentials are another family's necessities. It was apparent that well over half of the employed women neither counted on their paychecks to meet the rent or mortgage payments nor to cover basic household expenses. This only makes sense since most women did not earn anywhere near enough to be contributing a major share to their families' upkeep. But the money they did bring in was usually targeted for some specific, and in the mind of the beholder, important purpose, be it children's college expenses, supplemental food and clothing money, or the like. Particularly as children grew older, families felt the need for extra income.[1] In addition, as both employed and non-employed women pointed out, it is very easy (too easy, some worried) to get so accustomed to a wife's salary that the money she brings home becomes more and more essential. Most families spent up to their income, few had substantial savings at this point in their lives, and the more money women made and the longer they worked, the more their families spent and came to count on the extra funds to meet expenses.

While this seemed only logical to some, for others it presented a problem, especially for women who were followers. For the more a family comes to rely on an additional salary, the more imperative it becomes for a mother to keep on working and the more a wife assumes the role of breadwinner. In these more traditional families, it was acceptable for a wife to work only under one of two conditions. Either her job was viewed as absolutely necessary for family surviv-al or, if not, then her employment was accepted as an extra, as a way to get out of the house but not as a vital source of income. If a woman did not start out working for basics, it was critical to the family balance of power that her income remain supplemental. The more crucial her income became, the more it was viewed as a threat to the division of labor between husband and wife and the husband's role as primary provider. If wives were working in these families, their income was at times kept separately and used solely for special treats or savings. (This was true even though these families were not particularly afflu-ent; they were usually making around the modal income.) While there were only a handful of employed women in this situation, they represent one end of a spectrum. Though they are employed, their roles continue to be structured in very sex-typed and traditional ways.

At the other end of the spectrum, women talked of a different dilemma. Rather than feeling their husbands were discouraging them from taking paid jobs, there was another small group of women who felt their husbands were pushing them into the labor market, often despite their own reservations about combining child rearing and paid work. Most often, these husbands looked forward to the extra income their wives would bring in and to some relief from the pressures of being the sole breadwinner. Also, while the men were working, they saw other mothers who were successfully employed and felt that maybe their own wives could take on a paid job as well, particularly if they were already spending many hours each week doing volunteer work in their com-munities. As Blair Carleton described:

Sometimes when I'm doing all my volunteer work my husband says, "Can't you get paid for that work?" He would like to see me bring in a little money and he says he would help out with the children and the house and all that, but I really have my doubts. . . It's been a traditional set up where I've done all the housework and all the child rearing for so many years that I don't think if I even took a full-time job he would take over half the housework and half the child care. And anyway, he's away half the week, so he couldn't even if he wanted to.

Another woman who felt her husband would like her to take a paid job had just sent her youngest child off to kindergarten. Even though she was freed from child-care responsibilities for only two and a half hours a day (and less time every Wednesday when school let out early for teacher conferences), her husband had started asking her when she was going back to work. Although she would prefer to take some time before getting a job, she was feeling more and more pressured to bring home a paycheck. In addition, she, like many other mothers, recognized that money was often the measuring stick for how highly others rate the work you do. There were five women currently at home who were torn between taking a paid job and continuing to be full-time homemakers at the same time they were performing volunteer work. As Blair Carleton went on to explain:

> I think it would be better if I had a part-time job. I think my children are old enough that if I worked just while they were in school, just a half day it would be all right. I would be contributing financially to the family and I might feel a greater sense of self worth by being paid for something I did.... But I think one thing that I feel and most of my friends feel is that any paid job they're going to get would probably not be as interesting or involve the responsibilities that their volunteer work does.... Whether you want to go out and get a job as a secretary and earn a fairly low salary and do something you don't really enjoy just for the sake of money is a question that a lot of them have, I think.

While volunteer work will be discussed in more detail in the next chapter, in passing we can note here that volunteering was often considered quite personally rewarding, even if society doesn't value it as highly as paid work. In contrast to the types of jobs mothers would consider (part-time hours, flexible schedules, good locations close to home, et cetera), volunteer work continues to present an attractive alternative, particularly for women, like Mrs. Carleton, who can afford to stay home. She and other volunteers only wished that others would value their volunteer efforts more, so that they could feel better about their unpaid work and not so vulnerable to criticism by those who think getting paid is a be-all and end-all.

Having said this, it is still difficult to deny the importance of making some money of one's own. A paycheck is unquestionably one of the main rewards of employment, even when the money itself is not absolutely essential. Barbara McNair, for example, had a husband with a high-paying job as a personnel director for a large local company. Over her husband's protests and displeasure (since he had to do more around the house during the evenings when she worked) she had taken a number of part-time temporary positions. She recounted her reasons in this manner:

I wanted something to do, a little extra money for myself. I wanted to go out and buy a present for my husband and not have it be his money. I handle all the money in the house but he still makes it and it seems like I'm buying him a present with his own money. I wanted some money.

It was not unusual for mothers to talk about the advantages of employment in terms of the things they could buy for their families. As one woman summed up, a working mother "feels good about the fact she's bringing home money and can contribute to her family financially as well as in lots of other ways." The primary reason for taking a paid job and one of the main benefits of employment for mothers, just as for fathers, is the opportunity to make such a financial contribution. Not only does it feel good to bring home a paycheck, but it helps out with the spiraling costs of raising a family. Mothers' paid work, in this sense, is an extension of their family work.

Just how much of a contribution a woman could make to the family pocketbook was by and large dependent upon how many hours she was willing to work. Only one part-time worker earned at least $10,000 a year. About half of the remaining part-timers earned between $5,000 and $10,000, and half earned less than $5000. Only full-time workers made anything near what could be considered a living wage, and even then their earning power was way below that of men. About half of the full-time workers earned less than $15,000, while only a handful of husbands earned anywhere near this low an amount. Furthermore, the three women who earned the most ($20,000 or more) had husbands who earned substantially higher salaries. As a result, a wife's income was considered supplemental as long as a husband was available and working. Women expressed irritation about the well-known discrepancies between men's and women's salaries and they were frustrated by their low wages and the lack of better-paying jobs. Despite these constraints, however, and despite the supplemental nature of their income, they remained proud of their financial contributions and their ability to continue paid work even while they were child rearing.

Paid Work as a Source of Personal Fulfillment

In addition to the promise of additional income, another reason women worked is their recognition of the extent to which employment can serve as a primary source of personal fulfillment and satisfaction. A majority of women had some commitment to employment; they felt they would be employed for some, if not most, of their lives and they saw such employment as being inherently rewarding. Yet among these women, there were differences which account for many of the variations in how women integrate employment and family life.

First, there was a small group of women, all departers, who presented employment as vital to their self-definition. Deborah Hartman was one such woman. In her interview, she related what she found so important about her teaching:

> I find the relationships that over the years I've been able to have with my students have been long-lasting and have really become very much a part of my life, and to give that up would be to give up both the intellectual stimulation and the personal things. It's kind of like a passion that I have to do it. I just really love it. It fulfills my essence, my being. It sort of helped me when I wasn't able to have another child. I just didn't go into a decline because I couldn't have my 2.3 children. Teaching is really important and if anything happens to my son, I would have no children. When I think that, it's terrible to contemplate. It's terrifying to contemplate losing a child, especially when you have only one, but I always think I would have my 124 children a year. So teaching gives me enormous fulfillment and intellectual satisfaction. . . . And again, I think a mother's spirit is renewed by being in the outside world and involved. Working gives her a basis on which to live the rest of her life. You're only a mother for eighteen years—I mean, you're a mother for all your life, but the actual day to day contact only exists for eighteen years, and you can live to be eighty. So I think you have to consider your own needs for being a fully realized person, and I think you can only do that if you have contacts in the outside world.

There were only a few mothers who expressed similar sentiments, yet most respondents knew at least one or two other women, either among their family or friends, who thought about their work in these or stronger terms. Such women stood apart from the crowd. In the words of Jill Lucey, herself a full-time homemaker and mother of three:

> I think there's a few women who genuinely need to be working for career purposes. My sister-in-law is a lawyer and I don't think she could hack it at home on an everyday level. I think with all her education and everything she has to be working. Another person I know, I think she really has to work, there's something in her and I don't necessarily think it's wrong, but there's something in her that makes her have to do what she is doing.

For women like these, jobs are more than a way of bringing home some extra money; they are a part of their self-definition. They describe their commitment to employment as virtually continuous; unlike the majority of mothers, their feelings about the importance of paid work are not so dependent upon their stage in the life cycle.

Life Stage and Employment Commitment

While there were only a few women who felt as strongly about their current jobs as did Deborah Hartmann, more had felt strongly about some job in the past, and still more looked forward to a time in the future when they could immerse themselves more fully into the work world. It was not only that having young children decreased women's commitments to employment (which it did indeed tend to do), but also that a number of the most career-committed women had timed having their families to coincide with increasing feelings of burnout on the job. This was particularly so among those who had jobs which are noted for burnout; nurses, teachers, social workers, and the like. Even in their paid work, women tended to perform nurturant tasks, and many found that they needed some break from such human-service work; having a baby and taking time off for full-time mothering provided this needed time-out. Whatever the job, however, it oftentimes can be nice to get a break. As Helen Trilling pointed out:

> Actually having children and having to interrupt whatever career I had has been very good for me because it reinforced my decision that I really didn't want to be a secretary and now I have the time to go to school and to be able to get the education to do something else.

What this suggests is that women may experience different levels of employment commitment at different points in their lives. This commitment is dependent not only upon what stage of motherhood they are in but also how rewarding they feel their jobs are at any given time. Just as women think of child rearing as a transitory phase of their lives, they are apt to experience swings in their feelings about employment as well. Women who retain a high level of employment commitment throughout the early years of child rearing are in the minority. More often, paid jobs are viewed as very important at one time and not so important at another. As Lillian Henry explained when she was asked, "Looking back, how did becoming a mother and having your first child fit into your life?":

> I still feel very strongly that it was a good time for me. I felt comfortable that I had done a lot in my nursing job and that I had accomplished a lot there—I was comfortable with that. I feel comfortable that it's something I can go back to. And that I had really achieved something and felt comfortable with myself at the time I had my child. I think that was important. I didn't feel particularly frustrated, then, being at home; I felt it was a good time. I felt as though I had used what I had been educated for.

One time many women agree that paid jobs can be critical to a mother's well-being and self-esteem is when children are older and after mothers have spent some period of years at home. "Getting out into the world again" can be very personally rewarding, even if it can be difficult or even terrifying to take the first steps. Indeed, several of the women who spoke most glowingly of their jobs had been home for many years. They now judged they were ready to take on paid jobs without having employment unduly interfere with their family life.

In making the transition from home to work, going back to school was often the first step. As Tracy Palermo, the mother of six children, recounted:

> Two years ago, my youngest was in nursery school and I had an excellent neighbor who could help out if necessary, so I decided to take some courses. I've always been interested in the health field and so I took. . .an occupational course which involved six months of school, three days a week. It was from one in the afternoon until six in the evening and what it did was acquaint you with every field in the hospital. . . . It's amazing how hard you are on yourself. Anything less than an "A" is devastating, it's just awful. The kids really enjoyed it. They got a big chuckle out of Mom studying for a test because that's what they were doing. And I'd say to them, "Would you quiz me?" Which was the reverse of what had been going on. I'd come home at night and they'd say to me "Where's your mark? I want to see your mark. . . . I think they got to a point where they were saying, son of a gun, if she can do it, I can do it too. We had a lot in common. I was a little more sympathetic with the hours that they put in studying and their nerves about a test.

Approximately 10 percent of the women were enrolled in school at the time of their interviews. In all cases, they were using school as a way of planning and preparing for future jobs. One woman was in law school, one was studying computer programming, several were taking hairdressing courses and so on. All were looking forward to the jobs they would get upon completing their schooling. Even though the unemployment rate was high at the time the women were interviewed, few had reservations about their ability to find a job. They had chosen training programs in areas known to have openings, or they knew where they could be employed (for example, by knowing the manager of a beauty salon). In other words, the women looked carefully before they leaped. They went back to school with the explicit purpose of retraining themselves so they could compete in today's labor force. Although years at home are typically viewed as a detriment to career advancement, a number of women saw such time as helpful in allowing them to sort out their employment goals and chart the best course for the future. They were able to make welcomed midlife career transitions—an opportunity they did not feel was available to their husbands.

While some women went to school before taking a job, others just jumped back into work, usually starting out very part-time and then increasing their hours gradually as they became accustomed to managing the dual demands of home and work. Preparing oneself to take the "leap" back into the "real world" was often the most difficult step. Several women reported that they had spent months (or even years) fretting about whether it was a good time to start working and wondering whether they would be able to make it on the job. For example, Claire Dubois was a full-time homemaker for ten years. She had recently gone back to work as an x-ray technician, a job which she had held for about seven years before giving birth to her first child. She felt her fears and doubts about herself as an employee had prevented her from taking a job even sooner. As she explained:

> I guess you just get to the point where you feel like you do nothing since you're just a "housewife." And I was beginning to feel lousy about myself and feeling as though my education was going down the drain and...I thought to myself, if I ever stay home another ten years I'll never get back to my field. So when this opportunity came up I jumped at it even though it was very scary to get back to work because it had been so long. And I also think that's part of the reason I didn't go back sooner, because I was just very scared about it and unsure; I had no confidence. Now that I'm out in the field working, I feel really good about myself and I'm doing things that are important for me and for other people too. You know, I come home dragging, but it feels good, it's a kind of good tired feeling.

In many respects, it seemed that women who were out of the labor force longest were the ones who most appreciated their jobs. There were several reasons for this. First, such women typically felt that they had spent enough time mothering; they were comfortable that their children were ready to take on more responsibility around the house and would not be harmed by having an employed mother. They had accomplished what they had set out to do at home. Second, in addition to being there when they thought they should, the women often had spent a transition period during which time they debated whether they should get a job. This transition period was valuable since it allowed them to consider how a job would change things around the house and also to readjust their thinking about their lives and future. For some, this was a painful time. Increasingly discontent with being only housewives and mothers, they wanted something more but were not quite ready to commit themselves. They were finally able to overcome their fears and uncertainties about reentering the labor force, make the appropriate arrangements at home, and start working. Since women who had spent ten or more years at home had usually not counted on ever returning to the labor force, their success on the job meant a lot. They were proud of their accomplishments and felt their husbands and children were proud of them as well. Just as they had experienced the greatest doubts about whether they could get and hold a job, they expressed the greatest pleasures and satisfactions with their new role. In contrast, women who stayed out of the labor force for only brief periods tended to think of employment more as a fact of life. Although they did not experience the same apprehensions about returning to work, neither did they express the same sense of rejuvenation.

Paid Work as a Social Outlet

An additional factor influencing whether or not a woman got bored with being a full-time homemaker was how many other outlets she had and how many people she came into contact with during the course of a day. Some woman, like Karen Hurley, had families close by and lived in neighborhoods where there were many other housewives. They felt they got enough stimulation, company, and support without taking a paid job. As she reported:

My friends can't understand sometimes how I like to be home. They can't understand why I wouldn't want to work so I could buy the extras. They wonder how we do it on one income. Sometimes people look at you like you're crazy if you don't work. . . . Most of the time they ask you if you get bored, but I haven't been bored yet.

Other women, however, were more lonely and isolated while at home. In general, the longer a woman worked before starting a family, the more likely she was to rely upon the workplace as a source of friendship and support. When such a woman was first making the transition to motherhood, she often experienced a painful period of isolation.[2] She continued to identify with women who were full-time employees, and not the women in her neighborhood whose lives were centered around caring for children. At times, women who fell into this category went back to work right away (after only months at home, for example), in large part to reestablish contact with other adults. At other times, however, they stuck it out at home and began to seek out other mothers in the same situation and make new friends. The difficulties of this transition period have received a good deal of attention; one purpose of many childbirth education classes, for example, is to acquaint new mothers with other women at the same life cycle stage. Less well-documented, however, is the fact that the same kind of isolation can be experienced by a mother who has remained at home even though most of her friends and neighbors have returned to work. A woman who remains home longer than her peers begins to feel pressure to get a job, both because of the tendency to want to live up to group standards (including level of income) and because she needs new social outlets.

Not surprisingly, most women described their friends as being much like them. If they were full-time homemakers, their friends tended to be full-time homemakers; if they worked part-time, their friends also tended to work part-time. If they worked full-time, they did most of their socializing on the job, with work colleagues.

There were, however, a few women who felt they didn't quite fit into their social worlds. Either they felt uncomfortable with others in their neighborhoods or their lives didn't fit quite right into those of the other women around: they had preschoolers and everyone else had teenagers; they were home and everyone else was working, and so on. In addition, some just never saw themselves as homemakers; they eagerly awaited the time when children were school-age so that they could get back to their jobs and away from women "whose prime concern was children and their potty training and all that."

Thus, the workplace could always be looked upon as a social outlet, but whether women felt this was an important reason to seek work depended upon the social context in which they otherwise found themselves. The more satisfied they were with their social environment outside of the workplace, the less important were social contacts on the job. (More information on women's neighborhoods and other social outlets is provided in the next chapter.)

Additional Benefits of Employment

Beyond money, personal fulfillment, and social contacts, there are additional benefits which women derive from employment. As several mothers pointed out, paid jobs are more structured and, in a sense, easier than the unpaid job of mothering. Paid jobs have regular hours, set responsibilities, and an established system of rewards. Judy Laufer, the social worker who had recently quit her job to be a full-time mother, talked about the advantages of employment over child rearing:

> There's a part of me that would really prefer working, because it's just easier. What's expected of me is easy, I've got a job description. I get evaluated every once in a while and for the most part people are supportive and say, "hey, you're okay" and you get immediate feedback on your work and all those things. It's much easier. It's also nice being out and being able to go to the bathroom by myself.

Yet in explaining why she is currently home, she went on to say that these benefits could not make up for the time she would lose with her young child:

> Preference is different in my mind from absolute necessity and I feel like I've got enough maturity to put my preferences someplace else for a while, that what I prefer is not what's most important here. What's most important is the quality of care my son receives and I know the quality of care that I can give him.... Not working has made a big difference in my ability to relax with him. Everything doesn't have to be squeezed into certain time slots.... You can work your tail off and that's what I feel I did when I was working, and I was able to provide all the same things as if I were home. But the quality of what I can provide in a fairly unstructured atmosphere without a lot of time constraints is very different.

What this quotation again brings to the forefront is that mothers most often think of the benefits, and the costs, of employment in terms of their effects on their families. They work when their families need the money or when they feel it is appropriate to spend some time away from home. Not even the personal fulfillment which can come from a job is considered separately from obligations to children. Except under the most extreme situations, jobs are made to fit into family responsibilities and not vice versa.

Women rejected the notion that jobs, particularly full-time jobs, have no impact on family life. In many ways, nonemployed women were justifiably fearful about changes which would occur if they added paid work to their family work. The problems they imagined and talked about—the lack of time and energy to do the same things for your family, the lack of any personal time, the need to cut corners, and so on—were confirmed by most of the women who held jobs with long work hours.

Employed mothers, though, were not one-sidedly negative about the effects of their jobs on family life. Many felt their jobs had actually caused some positive changes in how things got done around the house, especially in terms of how much family members cooperated with one another. They did not claim that employment made no difference; they had no intention of being Super-moms and they had no delusions that life could go on as if there were still a full-time homemaker tending to everyone's every need. Instead, they acknowledged that the demands of paid work forced them to cut back on some of the unpaid work they were able to perform for their families. They were actually proud that they had been able to reorder their priorities and cut back on some onerous and expendable tasks, particularly in the area of housework. As one full-time employed woman said:

> I still do the cooking because I like cooking. My husband does all the laundry. We basically share everything else; I think what happens is that we don't do housecleaning. You can't be a good parent and a good teacher and a house-keeper, and so if something has to go, it's housekeeping.

About a third of the respondents could count on receiving substantial help from their husbands; most could not. Joan Levine reported:

> I have to do everything I did when I was home from nine o'clock on. My day starts at seven and I usually don't get to sit down much before ten....I wish there was an eighth day in the week. That would be a day I have to myself.

Women did not portray their husbands as chauvinists who sat around reading the paper, drinking beer, and watching television while they labored around the house. Only two or three were resentful that husbands didn't do more; in at least one of these cases, the husband was away so much during the week that the marriage was under a good deal of strain in other ways as well. The vast majority of employed wives felt their spouses carried an equal, although different, load. If they worked part-time, they saw it as fair that husbands would expect them to continue carrying the brunt of housework and child care. If they worked full-time, most often husbands put in even longer hours on the job. Except for the case of the one married couple who were teaching in the same school, full-time employed wives were home and available more than their husbands. Whether the demands of men's jobs were much greater, or whether it's just that these demands were seen as more legitimate than the ones from women's jobs is difficult to determine. Most likely, it seems that women took jobs which they felt would not make too many demands on their family time; their husbands were not similarly constrained. When it came time to do the family work, then, women saw themselves as more available and thus more responsible.

When they were old enough, children were sometimes counted on to chip in around the house when their mothers went back to work. If and when given, the cooperation of children was seen as a positive outcome of employment. Asked to describe the benefits of her job, one mother of two school-age children responded:

> In addition to helping the family economically, it has made everyone realize that we are a family, and everyone has to pitch in to make it work.

Deborah Sammett, the mother of two daughters and a hairdresser working over forty hours a week, similarly related:

> Before I worked, the kids always said things like, well, "Mom will vacuum" and "Mom will do my room," and "Mom will put my clothes away because Mom looks in here every day." Well, Mom doesn't do that anymore. Mom just leaves notes: I am your room and I am a mess. Clean me please. And lo and behold! Their rooms get cleaned up and Mom hasn't done it. There is a certain amount of cooperation between the two of them that goes into this new situation. Because Susan is only nine and needs a lot of help with her room, with Mom not there she goes to her sister a lot, which has brought them closer. My husband and I feel that my job has helped them in that respect. It has made them more self-reliant, independent, and responsible.

Several women also saw their children benefitting from exposure to other child-care providers, be it their fathers, babysitters, or some group situation. Lillian Henry, the mother of a two-year-old, had the following thoughts about the benefits of her nursing job:

> Ethan enjoys the bonus time he gets with Dada on the mornings that I go in to work early. Then my husband takes him up to the babysitter. He doesn't like us to leave right at that time and that lasts about thirty seconds. And then when we get there in the afternoon he's usually happy as a clam. He seems to enjoy the relationship with other children, which I feel is something that is important for him. He's gotten a lot out of that. I don't know that I necessarily think that it's good for children for their mothers to always be there constantly stimulating them. I think that children need to learn some of that on their own and to be put on their own resources for a while. . . . It's hard for a mother home

all the time not to be continually trying to entertain her child, and I don't think that's helpful for the child in the long run.

Other mothers talked about how they began appreciating their families more after leaving them for a while. As one part-time employee explained:

> The time you spend with your child is more precious. You appreciate your child much more. I know that I do, because I work. I see friends scream and yell constantly. Not that I don't scream and yell constantly, which I do. But I find that a child that has a working parent is not as nervous and neurotic as a child whose parents are at home.

Only a minority of women saw children as benefitting from their mothers' employment to this extent, however. The above two examples are the only ones which suggested that children, except under the most dire of circumstances, might be better off without full-time mothers. In contrast to the dozens of quotes which describe the problems and difficulties children encounter when away from maternal care, there were only a handful of women who saw children as gaining from the time they spent in alternative care situations.

While it is important to point out there were some women who talked about these additional benefits of employment, it is equally important to restate what should, by now, be obvious: these were minority opinions. The majority of mothers, employed or not, worried that employment can and does make things harder, both for women themselves and for their spouses and children. Because of their concerns, women either had decided to remain at home, at least for a while, or to tailor their jobs so as to interfere as little as possible with the normal routine of family life.

In deciding to put a priority on their maternal role, for at least the time children were young, mothers, in effect, took a leave of absence from the traditionally-defined work place. Even if they remained to some degree attached to the labor force, through their part-time work, they decreased their commitments to employment and careers. As even the more traditional women had come to realize, however, this absence or withdrawal was only temporary. What stood out in women's discussions of the tradeoff between employment and family work was their realization that this movement in and out of the labor force had some benefits of its own. It provided mothers with the opportunity, throughout their middle years, to regear, experiment, and refresh their outlets and their lives. Women have come to realize the benefits of having different jobs and different priorities at different life stages. At the same time, psychologists and developmentalists have begun to question the advisability of the standard one lifetime occupation for either men or women. Mothers appreciated having the space to make midlife transitions and the opportunity to take on new endeavors, whether the new endeavor was mothering or a new job. Employment was fine, in its place and at the right time, and so was the case with mothering. The opportunity to alternate these jobs was seen as a net benefit of becoming a mother, even if careers had to be partially sacrificed and earning potentials decreased. It was perceived as somewhat of a luxury to be able to alter one's course in midstream, to be able to take time-out for mothering and then to be able to go back to a paid job after time at home. Women were thankful for the women's movement and the fact that they have new opportunities in the labor force. But they were most appreciative of the fact that they now have the opportunity to combine experiences, to develop their potential not only as employees but as mothers and builders of their families and communities.

Notes

1. This is the situation described by Valerie K. Oppenheimer, "The Male-Family Cycle Squeeze."
2. For more on this, see Lydia O'Donnell, "The Social Worlds of Parents."

Part IV
Extensions of Mothering: Linking Families and Communities

7

Mothers as Social Agents

The words women used to describe their families and jobs resonate with their commitment to reserve enough time for child rearing and their perceptions of the importance of limiting paid work so that mothers continue to be there for their children. Yet the notion of being there is misconstrued if it leads us to assume that all of the work of mothering is done in the home. Although less frequently discussed and rarely given the merit it deserves, there is a whole realm of work performed by mothers outside the home, in their neighborhoods and communities.

This work revolves around mothers' responsibilities to provide their families with the contacts, services, and supports which they deem appropriate and enriching. It includes the undramatic but essential and sundry tasks involved in arranging a child's visit with a grandparent, finding a neighborhood playmate for a preschooler, making appointments with doctors and dentists, locating a summer camp, and making sure children are guaranteed positions in the local scout troop or soccer team. In short, this is the work mothers do to get things for their own. In large part, this section is about what resources mothers value and rely upon in their child-rearing efforts, and what kinds of services they regard as contributing to the quality of family life. Arising from their concern with meeting the needs of their families, however, comes an interest in maintaining the vitality of extended families, neighborhoods, and communities. This interest provides a powerful incentive. Because of it, mothers come to think not solely in terms of what they can get, but what they can pay back, that is, how they can support and replenish the very resources they draw upon. The section is also, therefore, about the ways mothers repay and renew these valuable resources. It is an examination of what mothers give to and get back from communities which highlights how women differ in what they give and get and how these different giving-getting compacts, in turn, shape women's lives and commitments, including their paid and unpaid work.

The Social Context of Parenting

Employment is not the only sphere of a woman's life which is affected by the demands of parenting and our culturally normative perceptions of what children need. Children also influence their parents "intimate and formal involvements with family, friends, and neighbors, as well as their more formal and less personal engagements within the wider community."[1] For example, when a child is born, parents often find themselves reestablishing and renegotiating ties with their own mothers and fathers; relatives, in general, start to play an increasingly salient role in the life of the young family. While not all of the women interviewed remembered growing emotionally closer to their parents when they became parents themselves, most did establish more regular and frequent patterns of visits and phone calls. (Although these contacts were not as frequent as some might like—slightly over 40 percent of the women felt that their parents would like to see their families more, particularly their grand-children.) Geographical distance at times stood in the way of families getting together, especially among the more affluent and mobile Green Haven residents. But, not surprisingly, virtually all the women expressed that in becoming mothers, they experienced new bonds and ties to their extended families.

In addition to their influence on family relations, children play a role in determining where parents live, by influencing their choice of housing style and location. Green Haven, as described earlier, is a town where couples go to raise their young; although some older parents stay on after their children have grown, it is not a place where the childless are apt to congregate. Claremont is more diverse, but here again, parents typically consider the needs of their families in choosing where to live. Families tended to reside in Claremont for one of two reasons. Either they had family nearby and simply could not imagine raising their own children away from kin (about 20 percent of the women in Claremont had lived there all their lives and more than double that figure had family either in Claremont or in adjacent towns), or they liked what the town had to offer—moderately-priced homes and apartments coupled with well-rated public schools and other children's services. The presence of children may not be the only reason which explains why families live where they do, but it is certainly a major contributing factor.

Then, too, where parents live—even down to the specific neighborhood and street on which they reside—shapes their experience as child rearers. Are babysitters readily available? Will there be playmates for the children? Are schools within walking distance? Are other mothers around and available during the day? If the answer to any of these questions is yes, not only are parents more likely to become involved in their neighborhoods, but their neighbors are likely to become important sources of support and mutual aid. Just as raising kids is easier when parents have family around whom they feel free to call upon for help, neighborhoods can similarly ease parents' burdens. Realistically, however, whether or not neighborhoods provide such support is often just a matter of luck, since there are a number of factors over which parents have only a limited degree of choice and control. A quiet street where children congregate to play may be the first choice of home-buying parents, but other drawbacks, including the cost of houses or their location, may prevent them from moving in. Several women who had recently purchased their homes mentioned that one of the major drawbacks of their new residences was that there were no other families at the same stage of child rearing. Recognizing this was a problem in advance, they had settled on their present homes since they were the only ones which met most of their other requirements, chiefly affordability. However, they experienced the lack of peers, both for themselves and for their children, as a real loss.

The lack of neighborhood supports can be particularly painful for women who have just recently quit their jobs to become full-time mothers. If other mothers are on hand, there is the opportunity to build new networks of friendship and support which can ameliorate the loneliness of being at home. One mother who was not fortuante enough to live in such a place had discussed her plight and feelings of isolation with her own mother, who recalled her days as a Navy wife. The best thing about her experience back then, her mother recounted, was having so many other women around in the same situation. Such group cohesiveness is clearly not available to all mothers today. Respondents complained about circumstances which prevented them from feeling part of a supportive neighborhood. Either they lived on streets with no other families at the same stage of child rearing (typically surrounded by older couples); or they had worked for so many years before becoming mothers that they had never before had the time or incentive to get to know their neighbors and therefore had to start from scratch building a local network; or they were out of step with the other women on the block—they were full-time homemakers and the others were employed or vice versa.

When neighborhood supports are available, however, parents certainly make use of them. Neighbors, particularly when they have children of similar ages, are turned to both for emotional and social support and for material help, through exchanges of child care, children's clothes, and the various other paraphernalia of family life.[2] Over 70 percent of the families in Green Haven and Claremont participated in such exchanges with other families who lived close by. Primarily because of their children and the needs of their families, parents became involved and embedded in their immediate neighborhoods.

Children's influence on the social worlds of their parents, moreover, extends far beyond relations with the extended family and neighbors. Parents and children are heavy users of local parks and playgrounds, town swimming-pools, libraries, and picnic grounds. Parents go places they never would have dreamed of going without children. When families go out to eat, they frequent different restaurants than do those who are unencumbered by the presence of children—a fact easily witnessed by dropping in at the McDonalds located on the Green Haven border any Saturday. In general, the leisure time and social activities of mothers and fathers are shaped by the presence of children. On the one hand, parents meet and befriend other adults through their sons and daughters. Upon signing her eldest child up for kindergarten, one woman reported being told, "The people you meet through your children will be your friends right through the rest of your life." More than five years later, she had come to agree with this statement. While some other parents related to the adults they met through children more as acquaintances than as intimate friends, even they admitted that these were the people they saw most frequently. On the other hand, the family unit itself is a source of entertainment and social interaction. Mothers talked of shared family times as being one of their major social outlets. Only a minority of couples went out alone together on a regular basis. Citing lack of money and time (as well as energy) as reasons, most instead went places together as families—to the beach, shopping, to the movies, to inexpensive restaurants, and so on. Especially in those families where mothers were employed, and thus experiencing an increased work load, there was a tendency to limit social engagements. It was the rare family who either entertained company at home or went out during the week, and many families had only limited engagements over the weekend as well.

In describing their social lives, many mothers made a point of emphasizing that theirs was not the type of family where parents took separate vacations from their children; instead, they placed a priority on togetherness. As a result, only a handful of couples (mostly the most affluent Green Haven residents) had ever gone away without their children and few mothers had been away from their families, except for the birth of additional children or other hospitalizations, for more than a single night or two. While not having enough time alone with their spouses was often mentioned as a problem, it was viewed as one of the necessary evils of child rearing. Perhaps, women thought, there would be time to be alone again when the children were grown. The vast majority of women placed a priority on families going places together, even as children got older and it became more difficult to convince them to come along. A few women expressed surprise that they had even come to enjoy different things because of their children. As one mother described, "I never could stand going to the beach before I had Sam. But now it's so relaxing since he can amuse himself just being in the water and being with the other kids. It's really very pleasant."

Because of children, parents also become involved in a variety of local child-serving organizations and institutions, from scouting to schools. Parents work as volunteer helpers, and, more informally, as the liaisons between their children and the institutions and professionals who serve them. Beginning with their initial encounters with pediatricians and childbirth educators, parents are called upon to meet and interact with dozens of service-providers. In parent-teacher conferences, at PTA meetings, and in the offices of physicians, social workers, guidance counselors, family therapists, and learning-disability specialists, to name just a few, parents and professionals discuss children's progress and confer (and occasionally disagree) on how families are coping with their child-rearing responsibilities. Parents donate both time and psychic energy to these encounters, and the number of different specialists and experts with whom parents must meet is actually on the increase. In addition to run-of-the-mill conferences and meetings, 15 percent of the families had at least one child who had gone through a "core evaluation," a diagnostic procedure conducted by the public schools to identify special needs and develop educational programs specifically geared to the requirements of individual children who are having trouble coping with the regular curriculum. As mandated by law, not only were these children evaluated by school staff, but their parents were called in to discuss the problems which necessitated the "core" and the family's role in supporting their child. (Unfortunately, in about half of these cases, mothers felt the meetings and evaluations were a waste of time; results of testing were inconclusive, recommendations were vague, and the child was left still being thought of as a problem. When things went right, however, parents were enthusiastic about the help they received and the progress of their child.)

The community involvements of parents must really be considered a two-edged sword: just as parents and children become more interested and involved in their communities, the community becomes more involved in monitoring the success of individual families and the development of its future citizens.[3] Simply put, adults become more visible in their communities when they become parents. Philip Slater has suggested that parenthood actually serves as a societal mechanism which prevents couples from remaining in overly intense and exclusive dyadic bonds. It does so "By creating responsibilities and obligations which are partly societal in nature, and through which bonds between the dyad and the community are thereby generated."[4] As illustrated by the numerous examples above, children play a major role not only in shaping mothers' employment patterns and schedules, but in exposing and involving their parents in the wider community and in influencing much of the rest of their parents' social lives and social networks as well.

The Work of Network Building

Simply enumerating the diverse ways parents come to participate in social worlds outside their homes takes us a little astray, since it becomes too easy to lose sight of the fact that the formation and maintenance of such social ties, whether they be to family, neighbors, or community institutions, require time and energy, or, in other words, work. This is the work of network building. The remainder of this chapter describes one aspect of network building which is particularly relevant to the lives of parents, that of being a "social agent". What sets being a social agent apart from the broader concept of network building is that it highlights not what individuals do to build a personal network for themselves, but what they do to connect and link others, their spouses and children, to the world beyond the nuclear family. For the most part, the work involved in being a social agent has remained invisible, even, at times, by those who actually put in the labor. For example, such tasks as being a room mother, Brownie leader, Little League coach, or Sunday school teacher may be part of parenting and family life, but they are rarely given their due, either in terms of the actual work entailed or the ramifications of such work for individuals, families, or communities.[5] Not only have we not paid serious attention to the amount of work parents do in this sphere and how it may enrich or constrain their lives, but we know little about how children benefit from their participation in the social life of the community. What do children or parents gain from being actively involved in voluntary organizations in their communities? What difference does it make if children are scouts, if they take music and dance lessons, if they participate in after-school enrichment programs? What difference, if any, does it make if parents are scout leaders, sport coaches, or school volunteers? Indeed, what difference does it make if a preschooler attends a mother-run playgroup several mornings a week or if children are driven to visit grandparents on a regular basis?

One of the only pieces of evidence we have which suggests that some activities do make a difference is a study by James Mercy and Lala Steelman which has looked at the activities of school-age children. They report that participation in group after-school activities is positively correlated with children's intellectual attainment.[6] Yet we know little about different patterns of children's involvements and how these patterns may affect not only cognitive gains but social development and integration into the community as well. Nor have we adequately explored the links between children's and parents' participation. Several studies point to the role parents play in fostering children's involvements, yet even major studies of time use, which chart categories of adults' paid and unpaid work, have not included the work of being a social agent as a separate and distinguishable task.[7] Parodies of family life may contain joking references to parents as chauffeurs and cub scout leaders, but more rigorous examinations have somehow overlooked the time-consuming nature and possible significance of these many varied tasks and activities.

"Women's Work"

Perhaps the real reason that the work of being a social agent has gone unnoticed is that it has been lumped in our minds under the general and ill-defined category of "homemaking," or women's work. It *is* primarily women's work. For example, as this study and many others have indicated, women are the "kin-keepers" of their extended families.[8] In their interviews, mothers talked of making phone calls to their parents and to their in-laws, and of how they have to remind and urge their husbands to keep in touch with their own relatives. Mothers, too, made arrangements for their spouses to visit their parents and for their children to see their grandparents; they bought the presents for birthdays, Christmas, and other special events; they cleaned the house and cooked the food for family gatherings, and traded off such jobs with their other female relations. Women also helped out with their elderly kin in times of need.[9] Most of those interviewed saw their parents at least several times every month (60 percent did so, and over 20 percent saw their families at least several times a week), and spoke on the phone even more often (all but 14 percent spoke at least three to four times a month). Respondents reported they had more contact with relatives than either their husbands or children. At times, women went to their parents and other kin for advice on child rearing, for help with child care, for a small loan to help make it to pay day, or for a major loan to help finance their down payment on a house. At other times, the women provided more services and goods than they received: they drove their mothers to doctors' appointments, they helped their widowed fathers and mothers shop, cook, and clean; they took care of brothers' and sisters' children in times of need; and so forth. But most importantly, despite what actual exchanges took place and despite who seemed to benefit most, even in the short run, mothers made the effort to keep in touch and, significantly, to keep their husbands and children in touch too. As one woman said, "I make my kids go every week to visit my parents because I think it's important for them to be with family, to see their grandparents, and to feel like they're a part of something."

In addition to kin-keeping, women also forge many of the links between neighbors and their own families. While husbands may borrow tools and lawn equipment on occasion, wives typically had more interactions with their neighbors, whether these included borrowing a cup of sugar, enlisting the services of the teenager down the street as a babysitter, or just chatting together while children played nearby. Given the fact that many mothers were full-time homemakers and so many others worked only limited hours, wives were home more than their husbands and had more time to be in their neighborhoods, and thus to participate in neighborly exchanges. In fact, the more hours a woman put in on a paid job, the less likely she was to participate in such exchanges and the less likely she was to feel supported by a close-knit local community. Seventy-six percent of the women who were homemakers reported that they saw their neighbors frequently and participated in at least occasional exchanges compared to 61 percent of the part-time employees and only 27 percent of the full-time workers. (There was also a community-based difference, with the mothers in Claremont being more likely to describe neighborhoods as places where everyone "knows each other and helps out" than mothers in Green Haven. Although there are a number of reasons for this difference, one stands out: More families in Claremont lived on streets where other families were involved in the same stage of child rearing.) Even employed mothers, however, sometimes relied on neighbors, particularly for advice about local child-care opportunities and children's services and often for help with occasional babysitting. If and when such arrangements were needed, it was mothers who worked them out.

Mothers bore the brunt of responsibility for learning about and choosing whatever community-based activities and programs their families used. In addition to shopping for groceries and clothes, mothers shopped around for family services. They asked other mothers for recommendations of doctors, day camps, and nursery schools: most of the women participated in some kind of mothers' network for information-exchange. They also made a point to read the local town papers to keep informed about offerings at the Y and the Boys Club, special school programs and the like. They visited different programs and rated their relative merits before deciding which one was right for their particular children. They filled out application forms and made sure to be there at the right time to get their kids into popular activities where space was tight. And, finally, mothers were responsible for making sure their children got where they were supposed to be and then back home again. More than half of the women spent between three and five hours a week chauffeuring (with driving duties being heavier in Green Haven, where the center of town is less accessible without a car). While some fathers pitched in to give children rides, particularly on weekends, mothers both drove their offspring around more than their husbands and were seen as responsible for setting up carpool arrangements when they were necessary. One Green Haven woman, for example, worried about how she was going to get her son home from soccer paractice if she attended one of the courses necessary to complete her training as a computer programmer. Although she didn't have to leave the house until five, at which time her husband would be home, she felt it was her job to arrange for her child's transportation. Her husband simply didn't concern himself with carpooling—it was construed to be part of her role as a social agent.

Besides getting children into programs and occasionally driving them back and forth, mothers saw themselves as being principally responsible for monitoring interactions between their families and the professionals and services they came into contact with. As Jacques Donzelot details in his historical analysis of the relations between families and the community, mothers have traditionally been the mediators between their children and child-serving institutions.[10] In both Green Haven and Claremont, fathers were usually invited to parent–teacher conferences and to join the PTA (less than half as many men belonged as women, or twenty-one men as opposed to forty-nine women). Additionally, fathers made a point of being on hand for special events, such as the annual school play, and when big problems arose (more often than not, they attended a child's core evaluation). But it was mothers who were expected to be there on a daily basis, maintaining contact with teachers and other service-providers and resolving the hassles and misunderstandings which sometimes arose.

Beyond this level of mediating work, mothers volunteered a substantial number of hours to local institutions. Whereas only 12 percent of the women had done any kind of volunteering in the year or so before they became pregnant, more than three-quarters were engaged in some volunteer activity at the time they were interviewed, and 45 percent were either donating regular time each week to a voluntary association or serving in some leadership position. In all but a handful of cases, women's volunteer work was directly connected to the activities of their family members. Mothers volunteered in private nursery schools and public elementary schools in order to see what was going on—to get a bird's eye view of their children's teachers in action—and because they felt their children delighted in seeing their moms at school. Mothers volunteered as religious school teachers and scout leaders because they wanted to assure their children's participation, keep tabs on the programs, and show their children the importance of being involved. Mothers even at times acted as conduits for their husbands' involvements. One mother who was a cub-scout leader for two years had urged her husband to try taking a boy-scout pack now that his sons were older. Another mother who taught religion classes while her children were in the early grades was successful in convincing her husband to try his hand at teaching sixth graders. While there were some avenues of volunteer work which were seen as legitimate for men, if not actually reserved for them (such as coaching sport teams), women, in general, were more involved than their husbands in a broader range of community activities. Not only were they active volunteers, but they were also more active in their churches and synagogues and in a variety of locally-based voluntary associations. Although the following chapter provides a more in-depth analysis of these involvements and their determinants and ramifications, it is interesting to note here that the more mothers were engaged in such activities, the more likely their husbands were to be involved, and, in turn, the more active were their children. This is what is meant by being a social agent.

The Importance of Mothers' Work as Social Agents

Having now illustrated in some detail what goes into being a social agent, it becomes easier to understand the importance of this type of work. By linking their families to the world around them, it is apparent that mothers are serving a number of functions. First, they are providing their families with those services which they perceive as vital to their welfare: they are getting what they want, whether it be a gymnastics program or sessions with a family therapist. Second, by mediating between their families and the outside world, mothers are attempting to reduce conflict and trying to insure that what gets transmitted to their family members is in their own best interests. Third, through their work and by their example, mothers are passing onto their children a way of interacting with their environment and a style of participating in society. And, finally, through their involvements, contacts, and exchanges, mothers are forming and solidifying those bonds and links which nourish neighborhoods and communities and make them work. By fostering children's involvements with their extended families, neighbors, and friends, parents show their off-spring the meaning and value of these relations. "If I show them what I do for my mother, then maybe they'll do the same for me," one mother explained. And by introducing children to a variety of community activities and voluntary associations, parents are training their young to make use of available resources and socializing them to be active and responsible members of the community. Since the time of deTocqueville, analysts of U. S. life have argued about the importance of participation in voluntary associations and their contribution to the continuing operation of our pluralistic democratic society. In linking their children to the community and performing their work as social agents, mothers are preparing youngsters to be future citizens. In sum, if husbands' jobs remain an accurate indicator of a family's social-class position in the community, and if we continue to identify and categorize families, in the broadest terms, in light of men's work, it is wives and mothers who enrich and augment this position with the accoutrements of a social life. By and large, it is women who actively embed their families in a vibrant and productive social network—one which both supports families in their child-rearing efforts and, in turn, one which contributes to the very foundation of what we mean by community.

Yet to state simply that it is women who do this work is to gloss over a number of important distinctions. Clearly, not all women do the same types or amount of work, and women do not always agree on what types of services and associations are best for their families. While one mother actively searches for a preschool program for her two-and-a-half-year-old, another may feel it is inappropriate for children to attend school until they are considerably older, say four or five. As previous research has indicated, for example, working-class mothers are likely to place a higher priority on young children remaining home with their mothers for as long as possible, whereas middle-class mothers are more apt to value early nursery-school experiences and seek out such programs.[11] Mothers also disagree on what specific chores associated with being a social agent are really important. Several respondents mentioned that they did not approve of chauffeuring children different places; the activities their children were involved in and the friends they played with were, therefore, limited to a circumscribed area around their homes. Other women searched far and wide to find special programs, even if it meant driving children a half hour or more into Boston and back every Saturday morning for a special class at the Museum of Science. Furthermore, in casting the work involved in being a social agent as part of the homemaking role, we have often assumed that such labor is discounted and discarded once mothers enter the labor force. This is not an accurate perception, however. Many employed mothers continue to perform such unpaid work. Using the example of maternal volunteer work, the next chapter provides a more detailed examination of how mothers consider the importance of their work as social agents and how they rank its priority in light of the many other commitments which compete for their time. By examining the ways women formulate their role as social agent, we can begin to appreciate the significance of this aspect of mothers' work, how it fits into women's lives, and the benefits which families and communities derive from such unpaid and frequently unheralded labors.

Notes

1. This discussion draws from Lydia O'Donnell, "The Social Worlds of Parents."

2. See, for example, Ann Stueve and Kathleen Gerson, "Personal Relations Across the Life-Cycle," Claude Fischer et al., *Networks and Places.*

3. Jacques Donzelot, *The Policing of Families,* provides a structural analysis of how the community, through such institutions as the schools, monitors and even controls the upbringing of children and parents' performance.

4. Philip Slater, "Social Limitations on Libidinal Withdrawal," Rose L. Coser, Ed., *The Family: Its Structure and Function.*

5. This argument was first elaborated in Lydia O'Donnell and Ann Stueve, "Employed Women: Mothers and Good Neighbors," *The Urban and Social Change Review.* Special Issue on Neighborhood and Community 14, Winter 1981, 21–26.

6. James A. Mercy and Lala Steelman, "Familial Influence on the Intellectual Attainment of Children," *American Sociological Review* (47), August 1982, 532–543.

7. For examples of such time-use studies, see Joseph Pleck et al., "Work and Family Life": J. Robinson, *How Americans Use Time,* New York: Praeger, 1977; and Kathryn Walker and M. E. Woods, *Time Use: A Measure of Household Production of Family Goods and Services,* Washington, D. C.: American Home Economics Association, 1976.

8. Ann Stueve and Lydia O'Donnell, "The Daughters of Aging Parents," Grace Baruch, Jeanne Brooks-Gunn, and C. P. Kopp, Eds., *Between Youth and Old Age: Women in the Middle Years,* New York: Plenum Press, 1984.

9. See, for example, Elaine Brody, "'Women in the Middle' and Family Help to Old People," *The Gerontologist* 21, 1981, 471–480.

10. Jacques Donzelot, *The Policing of Families.*

11. For a fuller discussion, see Lydia O'Donnell and Ann Stueve, "Mothers as Social Agents."

8

Mothers as Community Volunteers

To highlight mothers' volunteer work and the links between maternal volunteering and families' participation in the community is not to diminish the importance of the other ways mothers serve as social agents. Yet the example of volunteer work is useful for several reasons. First, volunteer work brings to the forefront the issue of how we as individuals and as a society value unpaid labor and the people who perform it. At times in the past, many mothers, particularly from the "middle mass," simply have assumed that they would be community volunteers for a portion of their lives. The housewife-volunteer has been a traditional, if stereotyped, role model for mainstream women. But is it still a viable or attractive alternative, in light of the emphasis feminists and others have placed on wages and workplace involvements? As it has become more acceptable, if not imperative, for women to take paid jobs, how do mothers weigh the advantages and disadvantages of volunteering? Indeed, what is the connection between maternal employment and mothers' volunteer work? In what ways is volunteer work personally rewarding, and are there ways families benefit when mothers donate unpaid hours of labor to the community? Put more crudely, to what extent are mothers ripped off and to what extent are they rewarded for their volunteering? Second, volunteer work, even more than the work involved in kin-keeping or maintaining neighborhoods, is quantifiable and relatively easy to report and record. The services donated through volunteer efforts are a little more clear-cut than exchanges with relatives or friends. It is easier for a woman to recall the hours she spent working in the school library last week than the number of times she chatted with neighbors or called her mother on the phone. As a result, volunteer work lends itself more easily to a fuller discussion and analysis. Third, volunteering is demonstrably and directly related to the types and amounts of activities in which children are involved. An examination of volunteer work and mothers' community involvements thus provides a lens through which we can look at family and community interactions.

Even beyond the above considerations, however, a final reason that volunteer work makes an interesting case is that it gives us a vantage point for viewing how families strike a balance between what they give to and take back from their communities; it provides insights into how women and their families frame the giving–getting compact. Little of mothers' volunteer work (at least during the active child-rearing years) is purely altruistic; rather, as a part of women's role as social agents, it is primarily predicated on the assumption that families can and do gain from such efforts. This does not imply a necessarily even exchange: families strike different balances in what they feel is necessary and right to give for what they take. The following discussion highlights these different balances and explores how they come into being, that is, how they are shaped by such factors as the ages of children and women's work patterns and employment commitments. What comes next is, in many respects, an extension of the argument which developed in the previous chapters. The more mothers described the labors which were involved in being social agents and the more they talked about the value they placed on these efforts, the more it became evident that their attitudes about employment and their paid work schedules are constrained not only by the visible aspects of mothering and homemaking, such as supervising children and cleaning the house, but by the more subtle extensions of mothering. Mothering is not confined to the home and being there does not mean that mothers are imprisoned in the confines of the nuclear family domicile. Mothers' work extends far into the community and, as such, we must start viewing its implications and ramifications through a wider lens than we are accustomed to using. We must consider the importance of mothers' work not just for children, but for our extended families, neighborhoods, and communities.

Volunteering: Pros and Cons

In *The Future of Motherhood* Jessie Bernard briefly passes over the pluses and minuses of volunteering. On the one hand, she acknowledges that volunteer work does exist which "approximates paid professional work, including research and report writing and complex administrative tasks." On the other hand, "there is also another kind of volunteer work that emphasizes love, tenderness, compassion, the simple desire to help" and is "essentially an expansion of the mother role." This latter kind of volunteering "permits a major commitment to the home but also a commitment of varying degree and extent, to an outside activity—church related, school related, community related." However, and this is the point she seems to emphasize, while "such a commitment may supply much of the satisfaction that a woman in the labor force receives...It does not, of course, supply income and hence a modicum of autonomy, as does a job or career."[1]

Most of our attention over the past two decades has been directed at this closing sentiment: volunteer work is not a paying job and subsequently cannot provide the benefits, security, or status that come with bringing home a paycheck. In keeping with this line of argument, six of the women interviewed expressed negative feelings about being called upon to volunteer. In the words of Shelley Mercer:

Whether volunteer work is important depends on where you are in your life. I mean, if you are at a point in your life where that's involvement for you outside your home, that's fine...But, in general, I think it's ridiculous, quite frankly. I think it's absolutely downgrading to women. It's so absolutely out of the realm and focus of a woman's role in life. It offers nothing.

Judy Laufer expressed similar sentiments:

I guess I have a real strong feeling about women and volunteering. I think it's a real rip-off. I feel that way about older people and volunteering too. I've seen the jobs that they come up with for old folks and they put all sorts of fancy names on what they do, but it's still free labor. And it really bothers me because it seems there's a certain group of people that it's aimed at, mostly women and old people. I think people should be paid for the work they do or there should be equity about who in society does the volunteering. If there are certain institutions that run on people volunteering their time, then let's set up the system so that everybody has a chance to contribute to it and not just certain groups of people, when, for the most part, their labor is not acknowledged.

The four other women who were opposed to women volunteering focused both on the nature of the work itself ("It's not terribly challenging or interesting.") and on the fact that volunteer work threatened to place unreasonable and unjustified demands on their time. For example, one woman reasoned that if the public schools were not involved in so many different arenas, from sports to sex education, they would not require so much volunteer help; they could do what they were supposed to do without relying on the free labor of mothers. Another mother felt that without spending what she considered to be inordinate amounts of time volunteering, she would never really be able to accomplish anything of significance, so she made the choice not to become involved at all. When asked whether they thought it was important for mothers to be active in the PTO and other child-related organizations, this small group of women responded with comments such as, "It's silly, they never really do anything anyway," "It's really only for the mothers to get together and I have different ways to spend my time," "I belong to the PTO but I never go—it's just so much hogwash."

These dissenters, however, account for less than 10 percent of all respondents. Not only did they express a minority opinion, but their lives were also somewhat atypical. Two of the six women were working full-time and one was a full-time law student whose youngest child attended a day-care center more than eight hours every day; together these happen to be the three women who spent the greatest number of hours away from their homes and children each week. While the other three women were not employed, they were unusual in the extent to which they expressed their ambivalence about being at home and their discomfort at being identified as full-time mothers and homemakers. All six women were departers; they were committed to establishing and furthering their careers to an extent unusual for the women interviewed as a whole. The three homemakers anticipated returning to the labor force when their children were older; the three employed women were already heavily invested in getting and keeping paid jobs.

A Portrait of the Majority

In contrast to these women, most mothers were committed to some level of community volunteer-work. For example, fifty-eight of the sixty-three mothers (92 percent) of school-age children were engaged in school-related volunteer work alone. Twenty-five percent of these women donated at least several hours each week to the schools their children attended. An additional 25 percent gave time, but on less than a weekly basis. In contrast, only one father was a school volunteer and less than a third of the fathers even nominally belonged to the PTO or any other school-parent group. About the same number of fathers and mothers gave time to other children's organizations, including scouting and sports teams (about 30 percent), but in over half the families where husbands were so involved, their wives had donated time first and later encouraged their spouses to join them in volunteering as children grew older and "didn't want their mothers around so much." In addition to these involvements, mothers were also active in their local churches, primarily because they wanted their children to learn something about their religious heritages. The majority of women were members of a religious congregation (73 percent), slightly over one-half attended services at least two or three times a month, about a quarter donated time on a regular basis each week to some church activity, and an additional quarter chipped in to help out when the need arose. Most often, women spent their volunteer time teaching religious-school classes, helping out in church nurseries on Sunday morning, and pitching in at bazaars and other fund-raisers.

The preponderance of time both mothers and fathers spent in community-related activities was directly connected to their child-rearing efforts. Only nine women volunteered time to nonchild-related organizations like the League of Women Voters, local museums, or the Red Cross, and only seven fathers were members of any civic or political groups. About a dozen women participated in various and sundry other activities, from book clubs to women's support groups but, by and large, the local associations and memberships of parents were related to their family stage and the activities and needs of their children. It is almost too obvious to report that not one mother planned on remaining a scout leader, room mother, or school volunteer after her children moved on to different ventures; only three or four women expected to move from child-related volunteering to other forms of community-volunteer work later in life. Mothers saw their volunteer work as a part of their role as a social agent for their families; when children no longer required such labors, most women expected to replace volunteer work with employment—either by taking paid jobs for the first time since they became mothers or by adding hours on to the (usually part-time) jobs which they already held.

To obtain a clearer picture of the extent to which mothers participated in volunteer work, the ways women reported being involved in such activities were tabulated. Women's involvements were then categorized into four levels of volunteer participation, as illustrated in table 8–1 below.

By relying on wives' accounts of their husbands' activities, it was also possible to categorize the extent of fathers' involvements, as indicated in the following table.

Table 8–1
Mothers' Volunteer Participation

Rating	Description	Number of Mothers
None	No evidence of volunteer activity or just nominal memberships; that is, if an organization was mentioned, the respondent described her activity level as "not active at all."	22% (16)
Low	Occasional participation in one or more activities, but no regularly scheduled volunteer time.	34% (25)
Medium	Active participation in one or more activities or limited leadership role in one activity.	19% (14)
High	Leadership responsibilities in one or more volunteer activities plus regularly donated volunteer hours.	26% (19)

Table 8–2
Fathers' Volunteer Participation

None	45% (30)
Low	23% (15)
Medium	18% (12)
High	14% (9)

Note: n = 66; 8 of the mothers were not married at the time of their interviews and they were not asked about the activities of their former spouses.

Cross-tabulating mothers' and fathers' participation reveals a statistically significant association between the volunteer ratings of husbands and wives.

Mothers' Volunteer Ratings by Fathers' Volunteer Ratings

	Mothers' Ratings	
	None–Low	Medium–High
Fathers' Ratings		
None–Low	67% (29)	33% (14)
Medium–High	35% (8)	65% (15)

$\chi^2 = 6.49$; $p \leqslant .025$; $n = 66$; missing data = 8

The more wives were involved, the more involved their husbands tended to be. Only one woman who reported spending no time volunteering had a husband who was involved in any volunteer work; in contrast, over half of the fathers who were not active volunteers had wives who donated some unpaid hours of work. The most active women tended to have husbands who were active as well. Fifteen of the twenty-three husbands (65 percent) who had either medium or high levels of participation had wives who were similarly active. Of the women who were most involved, almost 70 percent had husbands who put in almost equal amounts of volunteer work. In these families, volunteer work was a family affair.

Several questions arise from this descriptive account of the time parents spend volunteering. First, who are the volunteers and what distinguishes the most active volunteers from other parents in their communities? Second, why are so many people engaged in this type of volunteer work in the first place? What motivates them to volunteer and what do they feel they, and their families, gain from such involvements?

Who Are the Volunteers?

The extent to which both mothers and couples were involved in volunteer work was dependent upon several factors, namely their level of education; the ages of their children and their stage in the family cycle; and maternal employment-status, or more specifically, whether or not mothers had full-time jobs. Because of the extent to which they shape the volunteer pool, it is important to look at the influence of each of these factors more carefully.

Fitting our stereotypes which depict volunteer work as a middle-class phenomenon, a number of previous studies have documented the link between level of education and degree of participation in volunteer work.[2] Low-income, working-class mothers (and fathers) are less likely to be engaged in this type of community activity than their middle-class counterparts. To some degree, these data again support this correlation. Women with college educations were about twice as likely to be active volunteers (that is, to receive ratings of at least medium or high) than were mothers with only high school diplomas. This accounts, at least in part, for the fact that there were more active volunteers among the better educated women in Green Haven than there were among Claremont residents. (More Claremont women were employed as well, a situation which both reflects their lower-income status and influences their extent of volunteer participation, as will be discussed soon.)

While this class-related distinction is interesting, it is perhaps less important to focus on such differences than it is to highlight an important similarity, that is, the considerable extent to which the women interviewed, women who populate the American mainstream, were involved in volunteer work overall. On the one hand, unlike low-income and poverty-level mothers, the women had the time and resources available to be community volunteers. On the other hand, unlike highly educated, professional, and more career-oriented women, they, for the most part, neither saw volunteer work as demeaning nor as unduly cutting into their workplace commitments or the time they spent with their families. Instead, volunteer work fit into their lives, often quite nicely; they saw it as part of their work as child rearers.

Volunteering and Family Stage: The Beginning

Just as women felt the time they spent being full-time mothers would occupy only a transitory phase of their lives, they looked upon volunteer work in similar terms. Few women were active as volunteers before they became mothers and few expected to continue volunteering after their children reached adolescence. Only nine had done any kind of volunteering as adults before they became parents, and less than a handful of women were considering maintaining or increasing their volunteer hours once their days of active child rearing were over. However, just about all the mothers were involved, or planned on being involved, in some kind of volunteer work for a certain, specific period of their lives.

Typically, mothers did not become volunteers until their oldest child entered elementary school. (The exceptions to this rule were the few women who enrolled their youngsters in cooperative nursery schools and the one family who was eligible for Headstart, which places an emphasis on parent involvement.) Mothers with only preschoolers anticipated becoming volunteers and some were even excited by the prospect. Ann Ellman, for example, had recently spent a morning accompanying her preschooler to nursery school. She reported:

> I thought I was away from teaching but when I was in nursery school the other day observing I found myself saying, "Do you need any help? I'd love to come in and volunteer." I got the itch and sort of felt, hey, this wouldn't be too bad. Especially if I knew I was only going in one or two days a week.

Amanda Brown, also a former school teacher, expressed a similar urge:

> I'm looking forward to getting more involved. I'll be able to help out because I have worked in a school before. I've got six years of experience working in a school and I'm just very, very interested in schools now, from a parent's point of view.

It wasn't only former school teachers who expressed a willingness to get involved. Other mothers of preschoolers were equally sure the time would come for them to volunteer. As one explained, "Oh, I would always help. Every time they call me. We're not involved in that stuff yet, but we certainly intend to be."

Those mothers who had school-age children confirmed that such a time would come. They reported that their entry into volunteer work coincided with the year their oldest entered school. However, it was when younger children also entered formal school programs, even at times just nursery school, that mothers really had the time, space, and inclination to become truly active volunteers. Having an infant or toddler at home was a definite impediment to volunteering, but as soon as young ones were launched into the world, mothers had more time for everything—jobs, socializing, and volunteer work. Two very active volunteers explained:

> I've gotten much more active in the last two years since Craig (my youngest) started school. Both in the schools and in church too. Because we didn't get out so much when he was an infant. There was a lot of illness. So we didn't try then, but now we can get out more, so I'm taking on a little more responsibility.

> It used to be difficult when I had little ones at home...but now I'm very involved with everything that goes on with my kids. I enjoy it. I'm the coordinator for volunteers at the Adams school and I'm the recording secretary for the PTO....I have scouts every week for two hours and my husband has them every week for two hours, but besides that, it probably involves five hours a week between planning things and attending meetings. We've been involved since my oldest was in third grade—that's about seven years now.

Both mothers with preschoolers and mothers who remembered how difficult it was to combine volunteer work with caring for a young child suggested that perhaps something could be done so that mothers could start their volunteering at an earlier stage. "I think it would be nice for mothers who have youngsters at home and who would like to be involved to have some kind of swap time with other parents," one woman said. A few mothers were even apologetic when they explained they had not been volunteering time—they carefully explained that they expected to become involved as soon as their youngest became more independent.

If there was a standard schedule for when women started volunteering, there was also general agreement on how long it was necessary to stay involved:

that is, as long as you are raising school-age children. As Carol Santini, the mother of two and a part-time typist, said:

> I think my involvement will stay about the same because with two children, I'm going to do for Julian what I'm doing for Amanda. So, when I'm a room mother for Julian, I won't be for Amanda, but when Julian doesn't need a room mother, then I'll do it for Amanda.

Volunteering and Family Stage: The End

There comes a time when children don't need room mothers any longer (and, indeed, they don't want their parents around very much at all). Just as women with only preschoolers talked about the time they would start volunteering, women at the other end of the family cycle, with children aged ten and beyond, had started to pull out of their volunteer commitments. As children grow older, there is less of a need for mothers to be on hand, and this means, also, that there is less of a call for maternal volunteer-work. Mothers of older children pointed out, "He doesn't really need me there any more," often adding, "I'm not sure they really want me hanging around the school now." A number of these mothers recounted the ways they used to be active and how the time had come for them to shift gears and devote their time and energy to other occupations. In their accounts, it is possible to see both the transitory nature of this type of volunteer work and what types of jobs and duties mothers typically perform.

Janet Kelley has worked as a substitute teacher for most of the years since her four children, ranging in age from ten to sixteen, were born.

> No, I'm not involved now. I did library work at the school and I did hospitality-type things, planned coffee for meetings, recruited other volunteers, and all these sorts of things. I've done it—I've done everything you can name, but not any more. Everything you're going to ask me I've done—I've done my part.

Susan Klein is a full-time homemaker and the mother of three children, ages eight, fifteen, and seventeen.

> To be honest with you, I'm not in it right at this moment and I don't think I will get involved any more. I was up there with the girls so much that I think I've really had it by now. And there's a new group at school, they're a lot younger and it doesn't really interest me that much any more. . . . The thing was that the PTA I was in really floundered for a while. And it was like all the "oldies" had gone to work and dissipated. And then like for a year or two it was almost nonexistent. Now this other group has come in and taken over. A new, fresh bunch has come in.

Martha Kinney, mother of six, was working twenty-five hours a week as a key-puncher, a job she has held for the last four years.

The past few years I've been so involved I really needed a rest. There was one year that I was president of the PTA, taught Sunday school and did cub scouts. I look back now and think, "How did I do it?" I probably was involved in too many things and because I did so many and did them for a while, I got tired. I just didn't want to do any more of it; I had my fill and that was it.

Marian Farina, the mother of four whose youngest child is ten, has been employed as a secretary at Green Haven City Hall for the last three years.

I'm beyond that now. My kids aren't involved in scouting or anything like that now.... I felt I had done that stint and I didn't want to become a professional. Some people enjoy it and they become regional leaders, state leaders, etc. And they really enjoy that. I didn't enjoy it to the point where I wanted it to be a career. I did it when my children were involved.... I feel as though I don't want to do it any more. I think other people can do it now. This is the first year I didn't sign up to be a room mother. Whenever you join a volunteer organization, the work is always minimized. "Oh," they say, "you only have to do this, we'd love to have you." But if you want to do a good job, it's much more involved than you're led to believe.

One thread running through these accounts is that there is a time and place for volunteering—but after a certain point, the phenomenon of burnout occurs. This experience of burnout has implications both for individuals and for those local organizations which rely upon volunteers. As many women described, the supply of volunteers is not steady; the volunteer pool at their schools and churches had ebbed and flowed, resulting both in spot surpluses of volunteers and in periods of shortages. As Mary Neilson reported,

The librarian [at my children's school] says that ours is a super school, that we have enough people, that she doesn't even have to go looking for people. There are people who want to join and we don't even need them. When it came time to take inventory, she had all kinds of people down there and everything went smoothly. At her other school though, it was going to take her a lot longer since she didn't have many volunteers.... I think it's probably waves of people coming through that makes a difference. Who knows, in five years we may have a wave of people who are just not interested, who don't have the time, who have little ones, who work a lot.

Those women who volunteered when their children were the appropriate ages had to find graceful ways to pull out of their unpaid jobs and get started in new endeavors. A few women had become so involved that they found it difficult to cut back or pull out when they wanted to do so. As Joan O'Hara explained, "I think one reason I got my (part-time) job was so I could start saying no. I just wanted to do something else." Other women related that this was not an unusual experience: "I think that's why some women take on paid jobs, so they could get out of some of these things after a while."

Volunteering and Employment

The above statements imply that there is a natural progression from volunteer work to paid work. That is, after a period of being tied to their homes because of young children, women start venturing out into the community as volunteers; then, when children are older, they replace their volunteer work with paid jobs. Indeed, volunteer work has been commonly looked at as a pathway toward employment, and there have been a number of programs developed to help women learn to transfer the skills and experience they obtained as volunteers toward getting better-paying, more responsible positions in the labor force.[3]

This progression, while accurate in some cases, does not reveal the whole picture. It assumes an either-or situation: either mothers are employed or they work as community volunteers. Many mothers do both. Considering volunteer work as part of their maternal role, mothers took pains to fit it into their job plans and their employment schedules. For that majority of women who planned on spending some time being homemakers or part-time employees, volunteer work was just one more expression of being there. For example, in cross-tabulating mothers' volunteer participation by their current employment status, there was no statistically significant difference in the level of volunteer activity between mothers who were at home and mothers who were employed part-time. As illustrated both by some of the above examples, and in table 8-3 below, part-time workers frequently contributed considerable portions of time to volunteer duties. Forty-eight percent of the part-time employees received volunteer-participation ratings of either high or medium, as compared to 58 percent of the full-time homemakers. (While homemakers were somewhat more involved, it is unclear in a sample of this size whether this difference is due to their not working or to some other factor, such as the ages of their children, social class, or just random variation.) Only 16 percent of the part-time workers were not involved in any voluntary association.

The women who were combining part-time employment with volunteering can be divided into two groups which allow us to look more closely at how paid and unpaid work fit together. The first group consists of women whose youngest children were in the upper-elementary grades. They typically had started

Table 8-3
Mothers' Volunteer Participation by Employment Status

	None	*Low*	*Medium*	*High*
At home	16% (5)	26% (8)	29% (9)	29% (9)
Part-time Employed	16% (5)	35% (11)	16% (5)	32% (10)
Full-time Employed	50% (6)	50% (6)	0 (0)	0 (0)

out by volunteering and then gradually added on paid jobs to their unpaid work as volunteers. They did not stop their volunteer work when they took paid jobs and neither did their volunteering stop them from returning to the labor force. As children grew older and there was less work to do as mother-volunteers, in most cases these women were considering adding on additional hours of paid work. But, clearly, they did not see paid work and volunteer work as mutually exclusive. In addition to this first group, there was a second group of mothers who had been working at paid jobs for most of the time they were raising children. When the time came and their children got more involved in school and other activities, they simply added on volunteer work to their paid work and the rest of their responsibilities as mothers. Part-time work did not prevent them from being volunteers and social agents for their children.

The Implications of Full-time Employment

This is not to say, however, that employment made no difference. One glance at table 8–3 indicates that it does indeed. While part-time jobs did not interfere with mothers' volunteer work, full-time employment apparently did. Not one of the full-time employees interviewed was an active volunteer. Although it is difficult to draw conclusions from so small a number of workers, there are several reasons that full-time employees did not volunteer. One full-time worker was the mother of a preschooler and she thought she would probably become involved in some type of volunteering at a later point in her life. Two others had children who were older, and they did not feel they were called upon to do very much. Despite these differences in the ages of their children, the full-time workers did share one thing in common. None had been heavily invested in volunteer work at any point in their lives and only one expected that such commitments would require very much time in the future. Just as they stood apart from the other women by virtue of the number of paid hours they worked, they also stood out in terms of their lack of involvement in volunteering.

It would come as no surprise to the women who were volunteering that mothers who are full-time employees are less likely to spend time volunteering. It was pretty much an accepted fact of life that mothers with full-time jobs did not contribute as much as homemakers or part-time workers. Some women resented the fact that mothers could use employment as an excuse to beg off other commitments; they did not see paid work as an automatic and legitimate excuse. Others, however, were more sympathetic and understanding of the dual work load often shouldered by employed mothers. Single-parents, in particular, were excused from volunteer work without resentment (and, indeed, the single-parents in the sample were not very involved). Married women were often in awe of the work load such parents had to endure, even without considering the addition of volunteer work. When asked if they thought most people did their fair share, two homemakers gave the following responses:

No, I don't think people really give a fair share. For many reasons. For one thing, I know that many mothers are working now and that's their stock answer, "Well, I'm working." And I don't see how they could do it, work and clean house and be with their youngsters and all this. Then some mothers feel they're above it. "Well, you know, I have other things to do," [they say]. They must have the cleanest houses in town....And some, I don't know, I don't know what it is. The third category is the person who feels that someone else should do it for them. That's an interesting category, I find those people very interesting.

I can see that some people just wouldn't be able to do it. I think if you're working, it's kind of hard to expect a mother to take care of her family, her job, and then bake cupcakes, too. I can see why they say that the mothers at home get called on for everything. I think it's probably fair.

One common misperception among respondents was that only full-time homemakers were involved in this sort of unpaid work, since part-time employees also make considerable volunteer contributions. However, one reason women perceived that it is homemakers who get called on and who do more is that many of the women who were working part-time hours still really thought of themselves as being at home and available. Several part-time employees who were involved in volunteer work responded to the question, "Do you think most mothers do a fair share of this volunteer work?" in a curious way: "I know mothers who are working can't," and "If you are working it's awfully hard." The fact is that these very women were volunteering and they were working as well. And, if one is to believe their reports, they were not unduly stressed by these dual demands. But they thought of themselves as more like homemakers than like the women they see who are holding down full-time jobs. In many ways, this self-assessment is accurate. In placing a high priority on being there and on limiting the hours of their paid jobs, part-time workers line up on the side of homemakers. Motherhood remains their primary obligation at this point in their lives, and being mother-volunteers is one of the duties which they feel comprises the maternal role.

Notably, such obligations were felt not only by the most traditional and oldest women, the followers, but by many of the younger women as well, including many departers who identified with the goals of the women's movement. Although a few of the women who were most negative about volunteering were departers, there was no correlation between whether women were followers, straddlers or departers and their level of volunteer participation. Participating in the PTO, volunteering as room mothers, helping out at school fund-raisers, assisting teachers with special projects, teaching CCD classes, being scout leaders, and so on were all seen as part of a mother's job—at least for the passing portion of her life that she was raising school-age children.

Who Is To Gain? How Families Benefit from Maternal Volunteer-work

When asked if they consider the volunteer work they perform important, the majority of mothers immediately responded in terms of the benefits they derived for their own families—in short, what they get for their efforts. The reason most often given for why mothers worked both as school and church volunteers was, simply, because children liked it. Why did children like it? Because, as women reported time after time, it was one manifestation of mothers' being there. Consider, for example, the following three quotes:

> It's important to the kids to be able to say that their mom is helping out. That she's not just there sometimes, she's there all the time. It's important to say that their mom is there when she's needed.

> I think it's important because my mother [who worked full-time] was never able to come in and help out if a teacher needed extra hands for certain projects, and I think a child misses that. . . . It doesn't happen frequently, but if it does happen, a mother should be there because these are things children remember when they're older.

> Your child likes you to participate. It means a great deal to children when their mother is there and she is in charge. You know, it gives them a lot of confidence and they're proud. They know that you're involved. They know what mothers help out more than other mothers and it means a lot to them.

Elaborating on how she planned her volunteer activities, Janet Kelly described how it was important, both for children and for mothers themselves, to establish a balance between being there and having some time apart, to be able to gain from independent pursuits. In her words:

> I think kids have a tremendous feeling when their mothers are involved. I think it's good for the kids. But I think there can be that danger of doing so much for the children that you forget what your own personal limits are. So I think there is a happy medium. Kids should have their mothers involved. For instance, if a girl is going to be a girl scout for two years, I think it's important for her mother to be involved for one year and then have the child get used to other people's mothers for the second year. Thereby, the child retains her feeling that my mother's involved, I'm so happy and pleased, and, on the other hand, it gives the child a chance to learn that other mothers have different values and different rules. So the child becomes flexible.

Even in explaining how she limited her involvements, this mother spoke in terms of what was best for her children. Her history of volunteer work reflects this stance—she alternated being a scout leader one year with helping out in the school library the next, keeping her commitments to a manageable level so that she could fit them into her paid job but, most importantly, so that she could be there enough, but not too much, for her children.

In addition to making themselves available as volunteers per se, mothers also made a point to be on hand for special events such as school plays and recitals. This type of activity often took up a considerable amount of time, posing problems especially for those mothers who had full-time jobs. As Mary Kiley remembered:

> When I was working full-time, I would feel like I would miss out on some of their school activities that I would have liked to go to. For example, when Elliot was in kindergarten, they had this little Mexican festival and it was like at ten o'clock in the morning. I was very disappointed that I couldn't go to that. It's little things like that you miss out on. Of course, now, working part-time, most of the time I can go to a baseball game or some other kind of activity.

Mothers were often critical of those who did not go to such functions. Again, they focused their resentment on women who opted for full-time careers which prevented them from being there. Describing a couple in her neighborhood whose child-care arrangements she did not approve of, Barbara McNair made the following comment, "But they're both very, very career-minded. Like they wouldn't take some time off for things at school. I don't think that's right. A job's not that important." Excluding single parents and other mothers whose families clearly depended upon them for income, the women came down heavily on those they perceived as having some choice, but who they saw as making the wrong choice. As Laura Cuneo, herself working part-time, explained:

> There's always something going on up at school, a play here, a meeting there, the kids putting on their musical exhibition. I get time off to go see them. Most working mothers can't. I think they miss things. If I told my kids it was a busy week at work, they wouldn't like that.... Children want their parents or their mother to see them do things they think are important, especially if all the mothers are invited and nineteen mothers come and one doesn't. Things like that, children remember.

While fathers were excused from attending such functions because their work came first (a few made efforts to attend, but it was rare for men to go to more than one or two events a year and some went less than that), mothers were placed in quite a different position. Mothers' jobs were a legitimate excuse for not attending only if they provided the basic family income; primary bread-winners—men or women—were thus excused. However, women who worked either for reasons of personal fulfillment and career ambition or for supplemental family income were expected to participate; if they did not, they were open to censure for putting their work commitments above their family. Here again, women advocated the benefits of part-time jobs and flexible work hours. Despite the disadvantages of low pay, little employment security, and lack of advancement, such jobs allowed them to continue their duties as social agents for their children, duties which they obviously took quite seriously.

School Volunteering: Additional Benefits for Children

Another reason women put such a premium on being visible and active in the institutions which served their families went beyond the rather non-specific and intangible advantage of "children liking it." Mothers perceived that their families often derived tangible benefits as well. Although she was one of the six women who resented being called upon to volunteer, Lisa Ricci explained:

> I think it's pretty well accepted that if you're going to go into the schools and work, your kids are going to get priority treatment. A couple of times I could see that working at my kids' elementary school.... Like they had this great books program and it just happened that all the kids who were involved had mothers who were active at the school.

Other mothers agreed that by being involved in children's schools they were able to find out about such special programs and activities. Additionally—and perhaps more importantly—they were able to get an eyewitness account of what went on behind school doors. They then used this information to their advantage. Blair Carleton recounted:

> I think it is good to be involved because it helps you know about the school and the teachers and the program and because it familiarizes you with the setting your child is in. I can see that is helpful as a parent, because when I was in the library I got to see the teachers in action and I found a few that were objectionable. And I suggested that my daughter not be given one teacher because I felt she would have a very negative effect on her. Had I not worked in the library, I don't think I would have been aware of this teacher's problem.

Working as volunteers was a way mothers could keep tabs on both children and on their teachers. "Working in the library I at least get to see some of the teachers and some of the kids, like who yells and who doesn't," one mother said. It was also a way they could establish a line of communication between their families and professionals, so they would be prepared to act as mediators if and when problems arose. As Jill Lucey explained:

> I think the schools need to know, the principal needs to know, the teachers need to know, that you are interested enough to do the things they ask. Then, if you have a problem they are more willing to sit down and talk a little with

you and maybe offer a different solution to get your problem solved. I just feel if they can say, "Oh, she belongs to the PTO and does everything we ask," then they become more available to you.

Through their work as school volunteers, mothers strove to establish an ongoing rapport with their children's teachers and other service-providers. The importance of this line of communication between schools and families is underscored by the fact that just about half of the mothers had spoken with school-related professionals about some difficulty with their children. Usually these problems were not too serious, ranging from chats about discipline to discussions of why a particular child was not doing as well as could be expected. Regardless of how grave children's problems were, mothers relied on schools for information about their children, for evaluations of how they were doing, and for advice on child rearing. Indeed, parents reported turning to school-related professionals for guidance and support just about as frequently as they did to members of their own extended families, including their own parents and their siblings (over half of the families went to each of these sources for at least occasional advice). Understandably, the more mothers were around the schools, the easier it was for them to approach school officials if problems arose or if they were dissatisfied with the services their offspring received.

Mothers typically reported back on all such encounters to their husbands. Husbands were thus informed about their children's progress and problems, but for the most part, they had to rely upon second-hand information from their wives. At times, this referral process could cause tension and problems. As Linda Selby told it:

When my kids have problems at school, my husband comes home and I try to relate it to him. His first reaction is anger because one of his offspring is not faring well. And he's a perfectionist. I think if it were explained to him from a teacher's point of view, I think he would be less angry and more willing to understand the situation.

Unfortunately, as many mothers pointed out, there was not much either they or the schools could do to involve fathers more directly. Schools in both Green Haven and Claremont had made efforts to increase father-participation through early morning open houses, special functions, and special invitations to PTO meetings. Because of men's work schedules and demands, however, most fathers had little opportunity to get really involved. One mother reported her husband had gone to one PTO meeting but had been the only father there. His discomfort was compounded since most of the women present were also school-volunteers. They knew each other through their work. Not having an employment schedule which allowed him to participate in this manner, he could never really become a member of the "in group" so he stopped going to meetings.

(One full-time working mother reported a similar experience of feeling awkward.) PTO meetings and school volunteering was almost exclusively the province of mothers—and mothers who were either full-time homemakers or only part-time employees at that. The division of labor between husbands and wives was accepted as a fact of life, just as couples accepted traditionally sex-typed divisions of housework. It was not altogether a disagreeable fact either. Although some women were hesitant to admit it, because they felt others placed such a low value on volunteer work, it was apparent that many women actually enjoyed the contacts they made and their social experiences as volunteers. For them, volunteering did fit into a place in their lives. Not only did they see their children gaining, but they often felt they gained as well.

Other Community Volunteering: Impact on Children's Activities

Although the emphasis to this point has been on work in schools, mothers were also active in other institutions, particularly in their churches and in local groups such as the scouts. Here again, the major benefit mothers talked about was the enjoyment kids derived from seeing their mothers participate. But there is an important distinction to be made between these involvements and mothers' work in the schools. School attendance, after all, is mandatory. In addition, schools have a strong evaluative component; it is part of their job to chart the progress of children and, in so doing, to keep tabs on children's families. It is, therefore, not surprising that mothers perceived the importance of keeping informed about what was going on in their children's schools and of mediating between such an evaluative (and thereby powerful) institution and their families when problems did arise. Through their work in more voluntary associations, mothers accomplish a somewhat different purpose. By being active in their churches, mothers pass on to children how they feel about the importance of church involvement and religious education. By participating in scouting and helping out with sport teams and the like, mothers similarly assure and ease their children's participation; they soften children's encounters with the outside world. Mary Neilson reported on how her children were helped by having both herself and her husband participate as volunteer religious-school teachers:

> I have friends who say that their kids hate to go to CCD classes. I remember before we taught, my own kids would say, "Oh, do we have to go?".... When my daughter was in the first grade she went by herself. And she worried, would we meet her outside? Supposing we weren't there? The following year we had the same thing with my younger one, but since we've been teaching there, it's no big deal. I think they kind of enjoy going now.

Mothers got involved in order to make sure their children got involved. They saw children gaining in a number of ways from such experiences—children learned new and valued skills in everything from gymnastics to flute lessons; they increased their social contacts (particularly beyond the level of neighborhoods and neighborhood schools) by participating in programs offered on a community-wide basis; they competed in socially acceptable ways on soccer and hockey teams, and so on. There is a direct link between a mother's level of volunteer work and her children's participation in community activities. At times, this link is enforced. In order for a child to be a girl scout in Green Haven, for example, her mother has to be willing to volunteer time as a troop leader. At other times, however, it is more a matter of individual family priorities and values. Mothers who value children's participation in after-school enrichment programs are most likely to seek out such activities and to become involved as volunteers in those which rely on donated labor.

To demonstrate this link more directly, we can take a closer look at children's involvements in after-school activities. The following table illustrates the types of activities available to school-age children (the age group most likely to be involved in such activities) in Green Haven and Claremont and the percentage of families who made use of the activities on a regular, most often weekly, basis. With the exception of private lessons, the most heavily attended activities are also those which typically rely on some kind of parental support—religious education, scouting, and both publicly- and privately-sponsored sports teams. Most often, children were involved in not one, but several of these different activities. Of those families with school-age children, 44 percent had a child participating in at least two of the below programs; 51 percent had a child enrolled in three or more (see table 8-4).

While there were no major differences overall in the activities of children living in Green Haven and those residing in Claremont, there are some interesting distinctions which reflect the characteristics of the two towns. An example

Table 8-4
Children's Activities

Type of Activity	Total Families[a] (*n*=64)	Claremont Families (*n*=33)	Green Haven Families (*n*=31)
Religious Education	72% (46)	79% (26)	65% (20)
Scouting	45% (29)	42% (14)	48% (15)
Private Sports Teams	38% (24)	33% (11)	42% (13)
School or Town-Sponsored Sports Teams	38% (24)	27% (9)	48% (15)
School-sponsored Afterschool Programs	14% (9)	27% (9)	26% (8)
YMCA-sponsored	20% (13)	none	42% (13)
Boys Club	16% (10)	30% (10)	none
Town Recreation Department	22% (14)	30% (10)	13% (4)
Private Lessons	48% (31)	39% (13)	58% (18)

[a]These statistics are based only on those 64 families who have at least one school-age child.

Table 8–5
Children's Number of Activities[a]

One Activity	10%	(6)
Two Activities	44%	(28)
Three Activities	22%	(14)
Four or More	25%	(16)

[a]A report of the child with the greatest number of activities in a given family (including only those 64 families with school-age children).

of their parents' relative affluence, children in Green Haven were more likely to be taking one or more kinds of private lessons, costing up to ten dollars per half hour. More Green Haven children were members of sports teams as well; as more than one resident had told us, "Green Haven is a real sports town." For the most part, however, the activities of children in both towns were quite similar; for example, the Boys Club in Claremont served almost the same function and provided the same facilities as the Y in Green Haven. Both in types and levels of involvement, the children of the mothers interviewed seem fairly typical of the offspring of middle-income families.

The major reason for including a discussion of children's activities at this point is to illustrate one additional aspect of mothers' volunteer work, that is, the relation between children's involvements and maternal volunteer participation. The more active a mother was in community-volunteer work, the more active her children were in a range of after-school activities. Sixty-three percent of the women (with school-age children) who received volunteer ratings of "high" had children who participated in four or more regular activities a week. In contrast, only 30 percent of those women who scored less than high, and only one of the nine mothers who rated a score of "none," had children involved in as many programs.

This does not tell us, of course, which comes first—a mother's involvement or her child's participation. In fact, the two seem to go hand-in-hand. When children reach the age to become scouts, mothers learn about the program and begin to offer their services. The more their children then become involved, the more mothers become involved. Similarly, when children become old enough to try out for Little League, hockey, and soccer, their parents find out about the programs offered in their town and learn about what types of parent-volunteering are requested. As scouts and soccer increase in importance in children's lives, they also increase in importance in their parents' lives. There is something of a crescendo effect. The first year or so in a program, both children and parents learn the ropes, get to know other participants, and come to realize what is expected of them. If both the older and younger generation like what they see and want to continue the activity for another year, their mutual involvement and interest mounts, often continuing for several seasons. Then, when children are ready to move to different programs (or when they reach the age they no longer want their parents around), both children and parents decrease their investment in a given program and move on to new ventures.

It is during the period of heaviest involvement that fathers are also likely to be drawn into volunteer work, typically when children are eight, nine, and ten years old. It is not all fathers, however, who participate in such activities. As mentioned before, the more active their wives were in volunteering, the more likely husbands were to be active volunteers. In closing this chapter, it is appropriate to look at that group of couples who were most active, couples who can be labeled, in appreciation for their unpaid work, "community builders."

The Community Builders

What distinguished community builders most from other families was their emphasis not only on what their own families gained from their unpaid volunteer efforts, but on what they had a responsibility to give back to their communities. Community builders emphasized the importance of contributing to local institutions, of helping make them work both for their own families and for the benefit of others.

Fifteen families, or 20 percent of the respondents, could be categorized as community builders. In each of these families, both husbands and wives received volunteer ratings of at least medium or high. Cynthia Taylor, in describing what she and her husband do in their community, illustrated the considerable amount of time these families put into their community work:

> I'm a den mother and I've been an acting pack master for my son's troop for the last four months. All of the dens get together for a pack meeting. And I'm also involved in the school. Once, we planned a dinner there for 159 people which I'll never forget—I had to do it all on my own. I'm also the manager of my son's soccer team, the Claremont league. And my husband and I together coach the baseball team. . . . My husband also helps with the soccer team. He limes the fields and sets up the goal posts and that sort of thing. And I'm also an officer of the PTO, which meets once a month.

The division of labor among community-builder couples was pretty consistent: wives did more in the schools, husbands did more with sports, and the couples traded off scouting and church involvements depending on the ages of their children. It was typical, however, for both husbands and wives to have their hand in a number of different activities, often supporting each other in special projects and during times of high demand. Wives, in particular, were involved in their husbands' volunteer activities; in rather traditional female ways, they helped their husbands type notices and prepare flyers, they got the food together for the meeting of the boy scout troop, and so on.

When asked why she thought it was important for mothers and fathers to participate in such activities, Sara Johnson responded in a manner common to all the community builders:

I think it's our responsibility to support those institutions that mean so much to us and to our families. We do want them to continue and survive, and I think everyone has to give support. There seem to be fewer people now who want to do it, because of single-parent families who are overburdened. I think my husband and I are in a good position to do it.

Most of the community builders shared the perception that they were fortunate to be able to donate time. None of the women community builders were forced to work full-time, and none opted to do so. In fact, it was because they felt fortunate that they felt compelled to donate their time. This does not mean, however, that they did not have to arrange their schedules with care, since many were juggling multiple commitments, both to volunteer work and to paid jobs. Sixty percent of the women who were community builders (that is, nine of the fifteen) were employed part-time. They did not see employment, per se, as a valid reason for withdrawing from such activities. Instead, for the most part, they had taken paid jobs only when they were sure they would not interfere with their volunteeer commitments.

Like other less active women, these mothers did not plan on remaining as involved in volunteering as they were at the time of their interviews. Their current volunteer work, as well as that of their husbands', was related to the ages of their children; it was part of their child-rearing duties. Eleven of the women felt they would at some later point either be looking for a full-time job or for a part-time job which entailed more hours than they were now working. This high level of volunteer work marked a specific phase of these women's lives, the period they had taken out from full-time jobs in order to be there with their children. Community builders viewed volunteer work as a way to participate in and contribute to their communities at a time when their families were drawing on and making use of the resources which communities make available. (It is certainly possible that late in life, upon retirement from the labor force, these women will again return to volunteering more heavily; they would thus alternate heavy commitments to paid jobs and unpaid community work throughout their life cycle.) On the whole, community builders were active, busy people. Unlike some women who shied away from participation in organizations, they were joiners, and so, typically, they described their husbands.

During the course of their interviews, a number of community builders kept coming back to a similar concern—they did not see how mothers who were employed full-time could possibly do everything they were doing for their families and for the community. They did not see how it would be possible to balance housekeeping, child care, and volunteer work, while trying to work full-time hours. They felt there might be a few "superwomen" out there somewhere who could successfully handle all these demands, but they had not met many. However, despite this assessment of what an individual could reasonably be expected to do, even these very active mothers at times blamed themselves for a lack of energy and productivity; if only, they said, they were more energetic or they could learn to manage their time better. Then, maybe, they could really do it all. Realistically, though, they felt it was necessary to limit their commitments, and, as we have seen time and time again, limiting commitments usually meant pulling back from full-time labor force involvement. When asked how they felt about their current work loads and arrangements, these mothers responded positively: "I do what I want and it doesn't get to be a problem," "I can do what I want usually," and "It seems to work out all right." A full-time job, they felt, would not permit them to continue giving to their families and their communities; despite what they might get from such a position, they chose a different course. At least for the time their children were young, they wanted to be there, both in their homes and in their communities. Virtually all said they would prefer to keep things just the way they were (indeed, several women had turned down full-time job offers). Either full-time homemaking or part-time work was fine at this point in their lives; it allowed them the freedom and flexibility to be involved in what they thought was important for their families and to live up to their values and commitments. And, clearly, one activity which received priority was volunteering in children's organizations.

In closing, it is important to remember that this in-depth look at maternal volunteer work was only one way to illustrate the value women placed on their larger role as social agents for their families. A similar portrait could be painted of mothers' involvements in their neighborhoods and of the energy they devoted to kin-keeping. For example, just as in volunteer work, full-time employment decreased the amount of time mothers spent in their neighborhoods and the extent to which both they and their families participated in neighborhood exchanges. While making some difference, part-time work did not preclude neighborhood involvement to anywhere near the same degree.

Neighborhood Participation by Employment Status

	Little/No Exchange	*Medium/High Exchange*
Employment Status		
Homemakers	24% (7)	76% (22)
Part-time Workers	39% (12)	61% (19)
Full-time Workers	73% (8)	27% (3)

$\chi^2 = 8.01$; $p \leqslant .025$; $n = 71$; missing data = 3

Similarly, full-time workers reported that they had less time to visit relatives or even to talk to them on the phone. In contrast, the majority of mothers who worked part-time or were full-time homemakers spoke of the time they invested in continuing contacts with kin and with neighbors and of how they valued these relationships, both because of the help and support they received from such networks and because of what their children gained from experiencing close personal ties.

As is amply illustrated in the many examples above, mothers do not feel that their work is limited to the home; in integrating their children into the wider community and in demonstrating, by example, the importance of these involvements, mothers contribute to the social life of their communities and, by extension, to our society. Unfortunately, most of the work mothers have performed toward this end has been unrecognized. The major purpose of this section has been to draw attention to the work which is involved and how it shapes and constrains mothers' lives.

The women interviewed, on the whole, are fortunate and they recognize that they are fortunate. Unlike many others, they are able to make the choice to limit their paid work so that they can provide a home and a sense of community for their families. It must be emphasized that theirs is not a blind choice—virtually all the women were well aware of the sacrifices of career and salary they were making in order to spend a portion of their lives being there for their families. It is time that we, as a society, also recognized that we are fortunate to have such women—from community builders on down—who are continuing to make this choice. In the end, we all benefit from the hours and hours of unpaid work which mothers spend not only providing child care, but sustaining their families, neighborhoods, and communities as well.

Notes

1. Jessie Bernard, *The Future of Motherhood.*

2. Victor Rubin and Elliot Medrich, "Child Care, Recreation and the Fiscal Crisis," *The Urban and Social Change Review* 12, 1979, 22–26: Elliot Medrich et al., *The Serious Business of Growing Up*, Berkeley: University of California Press, 1982.

3. Judith H. Hybels, "Volunteer Jobs to Paid Jobs: A Transition," Report to the ACTION Agency under Contract Number 78-043-1008, May 1978; Herta Loeser, *Women, Work and Volunteering*, Boston: Beacon Press, 1974.

Part V
Conclusion

9
Giving and Getting

After mothers had spent several hours discussing their families and their paid and unpaid work they were asked, as a way of concluding, to assess their lives and commitments more generally: Of all their work and activities, what do they see as most meaningful and gratifying? What do they enjoy most about being mothers? What do they enjoy least? And, finally, what do they expect from the future? The majority of women took little time before responding to the first question in a manner similar to Amanda Brown, "My children have been the most gratifying. To me, that's the most important thing in my life. And, I guess, that's part of being a mother." Mothers obtained their greatest feeling of pride and accomplishment from making their marriages and families work, and from watching children develop into responsible and caring members of their households and communities.

Given what we have learned about the respondents' lives, such a response is not surprising. Currently in the active stage of child rearing, the women were devoting a considerable portion of their lives to homemaking and child care, even though most have, at one time or another, combined family work with paid jobs. In their closing comments, women talked not only about how they valued the time they spent with children but how they wished others would do so as well. Some appeared ill at ease when they described their commitments to parenting and their sense of reward from a job well done. They were aware of the unrecognized and undervalued nature of such work; they feared their attempts to describe their efforts and sense of accomplishment would sound like just so many empty platitudes. Even worse, they worried that their statements might be misinterpreted to mean they desire a return to the romanticized "good old days" when women were defined solely in terms of their relationships with others, as wives and mothers. Unfortunately, in our skepticism about the strength and survival of our families and local communities, many of us have become cynical. To talk of the importance of maternal child rearing or to emphasize the verities of home, family, and community, we think, is to take sides with those on the reactionary right who extol the virtues of old-fashioned mores while ignoring the social and economic discrimination women still face as well as the real advances they've made. Yet the message we should take from the women's stories is not that time has stood still, but that social change is most valued and effective (and even long lasting) when it is accompanied by some continuity, when we are mindful to conserve that which remains meaningful.

The women described here have struggled to find a workable balance between their personal needs and the needs of their loved ones, between the demands of employment and those of family life. I've referred to this balance as a new synthesis. In arriving at this synthesis, women acknowledge the priorities of mothering; what they, as mothers, can give to their families and communities and what satisfactions and rewards they receive back in return. At the same time—and this is the point which should not be missed—they acknowledge a welcome place for employment in their lives and the personal and financial rewards women reap from their involvement in the workplace.

Theirs is a reasoned, realistic, and well-tempered approach. If women reject the idea that it's possible to have it all at any one time in life—a fantastic career, a satisfying marriage, and the time to be there for their children—they also propose that the key to deriving satisfaction on all these fronts may lie in recognizing that it is possible to have different priorities at different times. There are times when a woman's first priority may be her job and there are other times when it may be child rearing. To assume that opportunities for labor-force involvement and the careers women build in their early adult years will diminish or distinguish their commitment to child rearing is to pass over the strength and resilience of women's ties to children. Similarly, to assume that time spent child rearing will negate the positive meaning of employment in women's lives is to ignore women's acknowledgement and acceptance of the importance of having different priorities at different life stages. In today's world, where women are no longer constrained to be child rearers, we find them choosing to spend a portion of their lives intimately involved in nurturing and molding the next generation.

Respondents overwhelmingly portrayed taking some time out of the labor force to mother as a positive choice, as a way of increasing one's experiences and developing one's potential beyond the confines of the workplace. As Judy Laufer concluded:

> I guess the most meaningful thing I am doing is what I think is important. I feel that the whole process of leaving my job and...raising my child is an important thing to be doing at this point in my life. I feel that I'm doing a lot of growing and that I will, in fact, be a more developed person eventually because of my decision to stay home for a while. And that's not just a way to rationalize what I may be feeling at the moment. I really do believe that ultimately this experience is going to be very important to me, as well as to my son. And it's something that's brand new to me; it's something I've never done before. And, in that way, it's something like an adventure.

Similarly, in answering the question, "What do you enjoy most about being a mother?" Natalie Green attempted to squelch the notion that she, or most other mothers, were so invested in their families that they would never be ready to move on to new things or to let go. As she explained:

I don't know how to answer what I enjoy most. My daughter brings me so much joy....I still go in every night and I just look at her and there's an intense love there. An intense love like something I've never experienced. It's very different from the love between a male and a female....It's an indescribable bond and it is not—I've thought about this a lot—it's not the fact that she is dependent upon me, because I realize it is my job to help her grow up and let her go. I know a lot of people say it's because the little ones are so dependent upon you and it's nice to have someone dependent upon you. But sometimes, it isn't; you get sick and tired of doing the mundane chores you have to do with the dependency of a child. It's just an intense love and the possibility of seeing her grow up and become a whole person, by herself....If I can do that, then I've been successful.

Because of the women's movement, with its emphasis on involvement outside the home, women were preparing themselves for the time when children would be older and families would not require as much personal care and attention. Most looked forward to divesting themselves of child-care responsibilities and to increasing their hours of paid work and investments in a career. Yet, at present, they felt they were doing the right thing by being there and by emphasizing the importance of mothering. Despite the "intense love" they feel for their children, this choice was not seen as entirely selfless. Mothers were sure of the rewards and opportunities for growth and development which come from placing themselves in such a position. In short, they felt they were being paid back for what they gave. Whether this was an entirely even exchange was immaterial and, in their minds, incalculable. Most respondents felt they had achieved a workable balance, the right synthesis of paid work and family work, and that, they explained, was what was most important.

It has become popular to argue that it is only through paid work that women will be able to build on their inner strengths and begin to perceive themselves as active achievers and participants in our world. According to this viewpoint, the domestic life may provide relational and expressive rewards, but employment is the key to instrumental ones, to "real" achievements and to a real sense of self-worth. There is an assumption of an inherent conflict between the individual success one can achieve through paid work and the mutual cooperation involved in the labors of child rearing and family life, between helping others to grow and distinguishing oneself. But are there ways to meld love and work, caring and striving so that this distinction becomes less salient?

Based on these interviews, the answer is yes. As more women assume that they will be employed for much of their adult lives, several things happen. First, women start to talk of mothering like it's a real job; they can compare its rewards and strains to other jobs they have held and to future jobs they expect to have. Second, child rearing becomes an active commitment. By being home with children or limiting paid work hours—even if it is only for a few years—women make a statement about what is important for themselves and their families. In making this statement and acting on their convictions, women have the opportunity to develop instrumental as well as expressive strengths.

Mothers, particularly at that stage when they are raising preschool and school-age children, most often feel they are doing a good and valuable job, one which demands real work and has the potential for providing a real sense of achievement. This potential may be diminished by the fact that society does not consider mothering to be an active, instrumental job and by the lack of appropriate child-rearing supports, but it is not erased entirely. As many women are now discovering, there may be times in life when employment is the most important, if not only, source of instrumental expression. But there can also be a time when the demands and satisfactions of child rearing can effectively and perhaps uniquely unite expressive and instrumental rewards. This is the time of life that has been highlighted in the preceding account.

To say that women recognized the importance of their work as mothers, however, is not to suggest that they feel society in general has appreciated or acknowledged their choices and efforts. Sara Johnson summed up how many women felt about their job as mothers:

> The poor housewife is so put down, not admired and appreciated, and I don't know why, because her job is just so crucial. The support of a family, the nurturing, the carrying of cultural traditions is so important and yet we haven't been valuing them and I don't know why. We've been valuing the work world and accomplishments there. And the accomplishments in the home are perhaps so much more subtle that they cannot be evaluated. Sometimes I get discouraged and my husband says, "Well, in twenty years, your rewards will come!" And I say, "Honey, they may never come and you need things to sustain you along the way, to keep you interested in everything you're doing, especially when you're going through times when everything seems a little bit of a drain."

Housewives, especially, were defensive about their decision to be at home for even a part of their lives. They worried about how other people would view their choice and rate their accomplishments. Even so, they did not retreat from their position; few were ambivalent about the importance of being there. Having a paid job made some, but not much, difference in how highly women considered the importance of their work as mothers. While eight women discussed their employment as being a major source of gratification, even in the majority of these cases, paid jobs were not placed on a par with their unpaid work as mothers, either in terms of how much work was entailed or in terms of what rewards could be derived.

It is possible to explain the subordination of employment to child rearing as a result of the lack of satisfying jobs available. It is reasonable to speculate that given better jobs—lucrative, high-status career positions—fewer women would be willing to put employment on the backburner while they raise children. Indeed, such employment experiences may actually change women's values and their approach to child rearing. While the potential for movement in this direction exists, the bulk of evidence seems to suggest this is too simple and unidirectional a model. On the one hand, there have been an increasing number of popular accounts of women executives and professionals who have been caught by surprise by the strength of their desire to have children and to be there for them. On the other, even in the best of worlds, only a few jobs are truly glamorous; despite a greater emphasis on the personal satisfactions which can be derived from employment, the bottom line is that most work is just that, work. Experience in the labor force actually helps many women recognize that the work they perform as child rearers is as satisfying and important as any job they may ever hold.

Several examples, all from women who were combining employment and child rearing, illustrate how mothers portrayed the primacy of their family work:

> I can't really single out one thing that's been most satisfying. I would probably say my marriage is the most gratifying, that it has lasted; having a healthy child is a close second. Work is something I enjoy and get a lot out of, but I don't feel any particular pride, or I don't know, sense of accomplishment. So work, that's a slow third.

> I don't think I could choose between my teaching and my son, they're equal ...but being a mother is the distinction I guess I would make. My son is just getting good...he's an interesting little kid. He's curious, he loves to ask questions. I can teach him anything I want.... I mean, he's really a companion, a friend, and I love that.

> This really sounds like bs, but I can honestly say that I have two of the most beautiful children, and I don't mean physically beautiful, I mean beautiful in the way they act, the way they conduct themselves and everything. I have never accomplished anything as gratifying as those two girls and I just hope I can see them through because they are very special.

A mother's pride did not necessarily blind her to the fact that family life does not always run smoothly. Women with only preschool or school-age children anticipated the problems they would encounter as their sons and daughters entered adolescence, and the parents of teenagers confirmed that some of these apprehensions are well-founded. A small group of women spoke of marriages which were going sour and others talked of children who were going through hard times and required special help and attention. But, in general, women derived a sense of accomplishment from dealing with such problems, from overcoming those they could control and accepting those they could not. As Martha Kinney, who had been forced to take a full-time job contrary to her expectations and desire after her husband became ill, concluded:

> Sometimes after Tony had his coronary and we were going to the rehab center, we had to see a social worker. I just walked out of there and felt like we sounded like Snow White and the Prince, and we're not like that. Sometimes I feel dumb and uneducated, and at other times, I feel like I'm a fairly sane person who can live reasonably well and have a sense of humor, and maybe that's all you need to get by in this world. I have no great expectations of my children, or of us, just to be normal, whatever normal is.

Just being normal, trying to live up to society's new expectations of women as individuals in their own right and as child rearers as well, is not easy. It requires a delicate balancing act. As with any great effort, there are bound to be problems and complaints, difficult moments and undesirable tasks. Whether or not they were employed, the major burden women pointed to was housework. If there was any part of their current jobs they would like to do without, it was domestic chores such as laundering and cleaning. When asked what would make their lives easier and better, most women quickly answered, "help with housework." Those families who could afford it purchased cleaning services readily and with little compunction. It was the one aspect of the traditional maternal role that promised few rewards.

Mothers felt, though, that most of their other chores were well worth the effort. They talked about the satisfaction they obtained from watching their children develop into thinking, caring individuals and of the power and sense of control they experienced in being there and seeing to it that their households were in order. Consider the ways women described some of the rewards of mothering:

> I like the challenge of coordinating everything and trying to have things run relatively smoothly. Having the kids do their homework, getting them bathed, and having them get out the door to school, looking nice—like I said, it's a tremendous feeling of power. I like to be in charge and to direct everything and I just think that's a big challenge. And when you hear them repeat something after you've told them a million times and then you think it's finally sinking in—that's a wonderful feeling. To think that you can take those little minds and mold them. I really, truly enjoy that an awful lot. I just think it's something a lot of people are missing.

> I just think keeping our life in order all together, that's most gratifying. Keeping a harmony and trying to make sure my son is spending his time well and has friends to play with—that's important to me. That makes me happy. And also, how I'm spending the rest of my time. If I can be creative and do some of my art work, that makes me feel good, even if I only get to do it for an hour a day.

Just being able to do it, that's what's gratifying. Keeping everybody doing what they're supposed to be doing; making sure everybody gets out the door and comes home at night and everybody stays healthy. Just the fact that everything is going all right. I get contentment out of that.

I guess I would say that I have brought up two children, that's what's most gratifying. They're not there yet, but they seem to be heading in the right direction, as far as being relatively independent and honest and upright citizens. I appreciate that I was able to have these children and expose them to different things in life so that they would have interests, even if they don't like the things I have exposed them to. At least they'll know what it is all about, so they can decide for themselves whether they like something or not, or whether they may like to try it at some other point in their lives. And I just appreciate that I had the time to do this.

These mothers were sophisticated in their understanding and awareness of what arguments have been made, for and against, women devoting time to motherhood. They anticipated our concerns as researchers investigating sex roles and women's work, and they spoke directly to some of the relevant issues: whether or not women have to sacrifice some sense of identity and autonomy to be at home with children; whether they would be unprepared for the time they would no longer be needed as child rearers; whether the satisfactions derived from mothering could equal those of the workplace; whether part-time jobs could provide any of the same rewards and satisfactions of full-time careers.

Employment was perceived as providing built-in rewards, including the satisfaction workers derive from meeting short-term goals and the feeling of validation women receive not only from bringing home a paycheck, but from being evaluated by others on specific and definable tasks. Women recognized that mothering has few of these advantages. Instead, its accomplishments are visible, at best, only on a long-term basis; there are no standard evaluation procedures and little formal acknowledgement of either success or failure. Even so, being mothers and acting on the importance of being there have their own powerful rewards. As two mothers put it:

Being a mother is the most gratifying thing to me. You know when you do something and you do it well. Like you're an interviewer and you really enjoy talking to people and you probably don't mind getting up to go to work in the morning because that's nice. And I feel that way about being a mother. And also, I'm a good worker and with every job I've ever taken I feel a lot of satisfaction in it and I do it well. That's how I feel about being a mother now.

I guess raising the children is a very gratifying thing. I'm starting to see the benefits of it more now than the hardships. You feel those more in the beginning. I think it's very satisfying. You begin to see the results of what you've put into it.... Somehow, when I was working, there were more positive reinforcements since you had job evaluations from your supervisors and everything.

While you're at home, you don't get those, but eventually you get the feeling that you're doing a good job.

If there was one theme that stood out in the women's closing statements, it was the desire for a greater appreciation of the choices they had made in order to be available to their families (whether they had "added on" a paid job or not) and of the work entailed in keeping a family going. Lack of validation from others did not appear to affect what the majority of women did or how they valued their work as mothers, kin-keepers, neighbors, or community volunteers. It did, however, affect their sense of how they were perceived by others. Women distinguished between an internal perception or feeling of worth and an individual's sense of validation from the outside world. Most had a strong sense of personal values and commitment, as well as a feeling of pride that they have been able to act on their perceptions of what truly matters in life, whether for themselves or for their families. But they were still troubled and often frustrated that others did not seem to share the same valuation of what they were doing.

This lack of validation is, in itself, rather interesting, since the women interviewed clearly are not alone in making such a strong commitment to mothering. There are many other mothers who have made similar decisions. Indeed, most of the respondents encountered such women every day. As women have pointed out for generations, becoming a mother heightens a woman's feeling of kinship and comraderie with other mothers, both through the acknowledgement of shared experiences and because of the networks of support and encouragement which gradually evolve. One might reasonably assume, therefore, that mothers would feel validated, but they do not. In addition to recognition from peers, mothers also craved recognition from those who have made different choices and followed different paths. They want their choices to be viewed as valid and worthy. As a group, the women did not feel that our society recognizes the importance or sheer amount of work which goes into maintaining families, which goes into establishing and continuing those informal networks of support which contribute to and enrich families and communities, or which goes into monitoring the interactions between individual families and the world at large.

Although it may sound trivial or platitudinous to some, it would be a disservice to the women who agreed to participate in this research if, in closing, there was no plea for greater recognition of the work women perform as mothers or for greater validation of their choice to limit labor-force involvements for that period of their lives when they are raising children. It would also be a disservice, however, to glide over the fact that such commitments do not come without some sacrifice—of wages, of status, of security, particularly if marriages break up or something happens to the children. To reorganize one's priorities around such negative possibilities, to go against deeply felt values and commitments to protect oneself from possible harm, however, was seen as unreasonable—a case of throwing out the baby with the bathwater.

In summary, the major aim of this study was to explore how women who are mothers today have sifted through and balanced in their own minds their past experiences and expectations, the circumstances of their lives, and the often conflicting rhetoric and ideologies to which they have been exposed. We have seen where women in the mainstream stand on the issues of employment and a mother's need for an identity as an individual and achiever outside the home. We have looked at how they perceive the strengths and resources of the nuclear family as well as the costs and rewards of being child rearers. We have examined how different women frame their notions of civic responsibility and how they, as citizens, decide what to take from and what to give back to their communities. These issues generated a good deal of discussion among the women interviewed, just as they have led to heated arguments in other arenas. This is not surprising since they get to the very core of how we define ourselves, both as individuals and as a collectivity, a nation of citizens and families. They expose and subject to question most of the important aspects of our lives—how we raise our children and what values we pass onto them; how we value participation in the labor force and, conversely, what value we place on the unpaid labors which are necessary to maintain our homes, neighborhoods and communities; how we draw the boundaries between our rights and responsibilities as individuals, as members of family units, and as participants in the community at large; and how we relegate responsibilities, rewards, and sacrifices both between men and women and among different members of the community.

What is surprising, however, is the extent to which most women agreed on their priorities and where they placed the balance between their own needs and the demands of others. They rejected the notion that children are just as well off being raised by someone else. They rejected the notion that the only valuable work is that which brings in monetary rewards. They rejected the notion that being a mother and homemaker is demeaning, unrewarding, unexciting, or unchallenging. They rejected the notion that mothering is all sacrifice and no rewards. They rejected the notion that mothers can accommodate full-time employment into their child-rearing responsibilities without damaging the quality of family life and without sacrificing other obligations to extended families, neighborhoods, and communities. And they rejected the notion that women cannot grow and develop as individuals in their roles as wives and mothers.

There will always be those who argue that these rejections are not real statements of choice, that they are made more out of constraint, compromise, and lack of opportunity than out of any true realization and awareness. There is some truth to this. Women accepted their primary role as housekeepers and to a lesser extent as child-care providers because they felt it was impossible to fight the status quo. But there is more to it than that, for the women made their choices and charted their lives aware of the many tradeoffs and compromises they were making. They realized their careers would be damaged by taking time off to be full-time mothers. They realized that part-time jobs are, for the most part, limiting and that, as members of the marginal labor force, they are subject to the ebb and flow of the market. And they realized that there are many who do not really see or value their unpaid work.

But choices are never really made in a vacuum. An individual's options are always limited, and making the decision to follow one path always precludes taking another. To date, we have not credited mothers in the mainstream with having an understanding of the ramifications of their choices or an awareness of the opportunities they have foregone. Many, if not most, of the women interviewed have balanced their decisions and made their choices based on such considerations. What's more, they do not merely passively accept sacrifices and willingly leave themselves in vulnerable positions. There were many examples which depicted the extent to which women were looking toward the future and preparing themselves for the time when children would no longer need them as much. The majority of women planned on increasing their part-time work hours as soon as their children were all in school. Some were retraining for the more lucrative jobs which they wanted when they returned more full-time to the labor force. Others, who felt their marriages were in danger, had started to increase their work involvements in anticipation of being left on their own; they were preparing for a future of self-sufficiency. Still others, whose husbands were ill, had begun to make similar forays into the labor force and were concerned with finding jobs which could support their families if and when it became necessary.

All this is not to say that mothers, even among this relatively privileged group of women, did not express any concern or ambivalence about their role identity or experience any hard times. There were clearly some mothers who did. Transition points, in particular, were painful: a homemaker sending off her youngest child to kindergarten wondered what type of job or volunteer work she should take, and how others would feel about her choice; a full-time employee who recently left her job and put her career on hold for the first time to become a full-time mother discovered she had to find new friends and make real efforts to become embedded in a social world which seemed foreign to her; a woman whose husband was just discovered to have a life-threatening illness was torn by the decision over whether she should stay at home with her daughter as long as she could or whether she should begin to find full-time employment, in preparation for the future. Women in such situations, it is hardly necessary to say, need all the help and support they can get. Just as we have learned the benefits of programs for displaced homemakers, there is a need for more formal support of women making transitions to other new life stages, whether this involves supporting those who are first adjusting to full-time motherhood or helping women retool their occupational skills in preparation for reentry into paid jobs. At the present time, not enough of these services are available. When asked what types of help communities could provide to them, mothers most often mentioned support groups and other programs whose aim it was to help women through difficult transitions. This is the one area where women felt they were not getting the advice, skills, encouragement, or support they need.

Other than this relatively modest proposal for more programs to aid women at these transition points, however, mothers seemed neither to expect nor want much else from the service-sector. On the whole, they were happy with the types of services available to them and their families. In reality, they are already getting and using quite a lot. Granted, the mothers contacted are not users of costly and well publicized public services such as AFDC, food stamps, Medicare, or government-funded day care, and these are the types of services we tend to think of when we enumerate what our government and our communities provide to families. But families in the mainstream make use of a tremendous and expensive array of both federally and locally-provided services and supports, from the income-tax interest benefit on home mortgages to federal aid to public education to the diverse number of children's programs provided by both public and private sources. In general, then, especially if we take into consideration the current state of the economy, it would be inappropriate to argue that these women and their families should be given much more. They are already getting a lot and they are, for the most part, quite satisfied with their share. In fact, it is not only through the more objective eyes of an outside observer that they appear privileged. For the most part, the women themselves feel grateful for the type of life they and their families lead. What they would like, however, and what they seem to have some right to expect, is more recognition for the work they do. This comes back to a point brought up before—the women desire validation from others that what they do is important and that their contributions to families and communities are valuable.

In implying that these women don't need additional services and in emphasizing the satisfaction and rewards they get from mothering, it does not necessarily follow that we (or they) must advocate or accept things just as they are. I think these data are misread if they are merely taken to support the status quo. The vast majority of women interviewed would agree that it is in everyone's best interests to continue the fight for increased labor-force opportunities for women, including the opening of new and more flexible career options and tracks. At the same time, I think they would agree that men's patterns of workplace involvements need to be reorganized and reconsidered every bit as much, if not more so, than those of women. Indeed, having witnessed how much women feel they gain from parenting, it becomes clear how much men, perhaps even more than women, are confined and limited by their roles. Men's jobs and work hours prevent them from spending much time with their children; in addition, their role as primary breadwinners and the dictates of male careers often prevent them from making the midlife transitions women apparently so appreciate. A number of mothers mentioned that, taking everything into consideration, they thought their husbands really had a harder time than they did; it was fathers' lives that seemed more constrained by the ways occupations and careers (as well as domestic life) continue to be structured. Clearly, we must continue to work for changes which allow women greater accesss to positions of power in the labor force, even if they take some time off for full-time mothering, and for opportunities which allow men greater access to the rewards and pleasures of parenting.

Similarly, there are many women today who do not have the opportunity to choose to stay home with their young children or limit their paid work hours. In fact, public policy has been moving in the direction of forcing low-income mothers, even those with preschool children, to take jobs in order to receive any government subsidies or benefits. The wisdom of such tactics must be reconsidered. It is not only a question of limiting the options available to women and possibly forcing them to do things which go against strongly held commitments to maternal child rearing. It is also that mothers who are at home or who can afford to limit their work hours are able to do things for their children—to mediate between their families and communities—that full-time employees are not. By forcing poor mothers to work rather than helping them be more effective social agents for their children, for example, we are affecting children's as well as parents',lives and may be increasing the divisions between families in poverty and those in the mainstream. By being there, middle-income mothers get things for their families. They learn how to manipulate and use the system, and also how to replenish and pay back the resources they draw upon. These are valuable lessons and ones which should not be limited to only those of us who are most fortunate.

In working toward new arrangements and designing our public policies, therefore, we need to be careful what we choose to dismiss lightly and what activities and commitments we sacrifice. If anything, the mothers who took part in this study spoke to the importance of child rearing, of family life, and of maintaining a satisfactory level of community. Their warning was clear: in pursuing goals of equality and in opening up new avenues to both men and women, it is important to remember the satisfactions, pleasures, and positive ramifications of maintaining some more traditional responsibilities as well.

In conclusion, it is necessary to look beyond the present and address the question of how things will—or should—be different in times to come. The average age of women in this sample was thirty-seven. I set out to interview women in midlife, women who only experienced many of the social changes of the last several decades in adulthood, after many of their values and behaviors were already formed. They are women who did not have all the opportunities available to them which are open to the younger generation today. Among the women, though, there were those who had aligned themselves with the women's movement and who felt that they have been privy to new avenues of participation in the labor force and new ways of combining their roles as wives, mothers, and employees. But these women joined their more traditional sisters in emphasizing the importance of mothering in women's lives and in realizing what we all—our children, our families, and our communities—stand to gain from women's continuing commitments to being there. If the next generation recognizes the value, importance, and place of all the tasks and responsibilities we have lumped together under the rubric of "mother's work," we can all rest easier about the survival and future of our families and our local communities.

Index

About the Author

Lydia N. O'Donnell is a research associate at the Wellesley College Center for Research on Women. A former day-care center administrator, she is a graduate of the University of Pennsylvania and has received Ed.M. and Ed.D. degrees from the Harvard University Graduate School of Education. At Wellesley, she is currently completing a National Institute of Mental Health postdoctoral fellowship in the area of sex roles and mental health. She is the author of a number of publications in the areas of child care, parenting, and children's activities.